THE CHURCH

Rights and Responsibilities of the Believer

ZACHARIAS TANEE FOMUM

https://ztfbooks.com
ztfbooks@cmfionline.org

CONTENTS

CHAPTER TEN

PREFACE

In this message, we have looked at the rights, privileges and responsibilities of the believer within the context of the church. The message is simply a systematic exposition of the scriptures in the book of Ephesians.

The book of Ephesians, on which this study is based, was not written to independent individuals. It was written to the church. All of God's power is available to us in the context of the church.

Total power was manifested in Christ, the Head of the church. After that, God has purposed that His total power would be manifested not in the arm, foot or eye, but in the whole body; the body of Christ, which is the church.

The church is not a human creation. The church is not a creation of the apostles. The church is the creation of the Triune God. The church was in the mind of the Triune God—Father, Son and Holy Spirit – from the very beginning.

The purposes of God are tied to the church. The exaltation of Christ has the church in view. It has nothing else in view. In a sense, He has only the church in mind. He does not have individual believers in mind, even if they are very consecrated and holy.

Unless I find my place in the church, in the local context, I have missed it all; I am out of His purpose. Unless I see myself, my character, and my work, in the context of that which God has set Christ as head, I have missed it. It is from this perspective that the Lord Jesus could say,

> ... *I will build my church, and the powers of death shall not prevail against it* (Matthew 16:16).

It may be good for us to begin by looking briefly at what the Bible says about the Church:

- The Church is the dwelling place of God in the Spirit (Ephesians 2:22). The Lord Jesus said, *If a man loves me, he will keep my word, and my Father will love him, and we will come to him, and make our home with him* (John 14:23).
- The church is the dwelling place of the Holy Spirit; *Do you not know that you are God's temple and that God's Spirit dwells in you? If anyone destroys God's temple, God will destroy him. For God's temple is holy, and that temple you are* (1Corinthians 3:16-17). *Do you not know that your body is the temple of the Holy Spirit within you, which you have from God? You are not your own* (1Corinthians 6:19).
- The church is the body of Christ. The Bible says, *And he has put all things under his feet and has made him the head over all things for the church, which is his body, the fullness of him who fills all in all* (Ephesians 1:22-23).
- The church is the family of God. The Bible says, *But to all who received him, who believed in his name, he gave power to become children of God; who were born, not of blood nor of the will of the flesh nor of the will of man, but of God* (John 1:12-13).
- The church is made up of:

1. The adopted sons of God (Galatians 4:5).
2. The children of the kingdom (Matthew 13:38).
3. The followers of God (Ephesians 5:1).
4. Heirs of God (Romans 8:17).

5. Co-heirs with Christ (Romans 8:17).
6. Sons of God (Romans 8:14).

CHAPTER ONE

Blessed be the God and Father of our Lord Jesus Christ, who has blessed us in Christ with every spiritual blessing in the heavenly places, even as he chose us in him before the foundation of the world, that we should be holy and blameless before him. He destined us in love to be his sons through Jesus Christ, according to the purpose of his will, to the praise of his glorious grace which he freely bestowed on us in the Beloved.

— *EPHESIANS 1:3-6*

BLESSED BE THE GOD AND FATHER OF OUR LORD JESUS CHRIST

*T*he apostle begins by saying, "Blessed be the God and Father of our Lord Jesus Christ." Why? Because He has done something: He has blessed us in Christ with every spiritual blessing in the heavenly places. The blessed one takes delight in praising God.

However, God is blessed whether we bless Him or not. He is great whether we praise Him or not. Even if we do not worship Him, He is worthy of worship. Even if we do not proclaim His majesty, He is majestic. Some people think that He will be poorer if they do not praise Him. There is a sense in which we cannot add to His greatness by whatever we do. He is just great. You praise Him for your own good.

Here, Paul was writing to the saints. They were saints because they had come into a vital contact with the Lord Jesus Christ. All who come into a vital contact with the Lord Jesus Christ are saints. Even if they believed only very recently, they are saints. At the very second when they enter into vital fellowship with the Lord Jesus Christ, they become saints. God has blessed them. But He has blessed them not in themselves, not in a system, not in an organisation, not in a philosophy. He has blessed them in a person—in Christ.

2

BLESSED IN CHRIST

*W*hat did God do? He took us and put us in Christ and, by being in Christ, we are blessed. Everyone in Christ is blessed. All who find themselves in Christ are blessed. There is not a single person in Christ who is not blessed. The greatest blessing a person can enter into is to be found in Christ.

When a person plunges into Christ, he has plunged into blessing. Yes, God has blessed us in Christ. What is the dimension, extent to which He has blessed us? With what has He blessed us? The Bible says,

with every spiritual blessing in the heavenly realms.

You are blessed in Christ. Take your position in Christ and thereby enter into your blessing. Are you in Christ? Therefore you are blessed, even if you are only a week old in Him. You are the blessed one, in Christ. Remember that you are blessed with all spiritual blessings in the heavenly places. It is all, not some. Notice that it is not all the spiritual blessings in earthly places. No, – in the heavenly places.

3

SPIRITUAL BLESSING IN THE HEAVENLY PLACES

The heavenly places talk of that sphere where God has unchallenged authority, and where His blessings flow unhindered. It is where all the treasures of God are. In kingdoms, there is a treasure house. If there is anything of worth, it is kept there. God also has a treasure house in the heavenly places. The Bible says that God has blessed us in the heavenly realms with all that is found in the treasure house of God.

What it means is that there is no spiritual blessing that God has kept from us who believe in Christ. God has taken all the spiritual blessings in the heavenly places and put them in Christ. Then, He has given us Christ, thereby giving us all. We have all in Christ. God in Christ is not a retailer. He has given us everything as a whole in Christ. We have all to the full in Christ.

Jesus is the great treasure. When a man sells everything he has, he buys that treasure in its totality as well (Matthew 13:44-46). God has put all spiritual blessings in Christ so that all who have Christ have everything.

Everything is ours in Christ. Those who are in Christ have come to fullness of life in Him.

Jesus Christ is God's all. Therefore, in giving us Christ, God has held nothing back. This is a very humbling truth and the implications are very far-reaching. The first response to such a blessing ought to be worship.

You lack no spiritual blessing. There is no blessing in the heavenly realms, which you do not have. Why? You have Christ. The wealth of the Christian life lies in the exploration of this "mine," that is Christ. It is as if you have been offered a very massive gold mine for free. It is so vast that you may spend twenty, thirty years just exploring to see what is in there.

Those who are fully in Christ have realised that the more satisfaction they get, the more they want to dig into Him more and more. When one begins the walk in Christ, it is as if God the Holy Spirit takes him on a revelation tour of His riches in Christ. The depth, breadth and height of these riches are unfathomable.

Outside of Christ, a person is absolutely bankrupt; he has nothing—really nothing. But in Christ, he has everything. Here then lies the miracle that takes place in salvation. When people respond to Christ, they have exchanged their poverty for riches without limit. They are in for every spiritual blessing in the heavenly places.

Are you a believer in Christ? If you are, then stop behaving like a beggar. I once read the story of a woman who put a lot of money in a Bible and gave it to her son. This was the only inheritance she left her son when she was dying. The son was offended and said, "This terrible woman; all she has left for me is a Bible." He closed it, threw it aside and lived in abject poverty for thirty years. After those thirty years, he opened the Bible and found out that there was enough for him to have lived in absolute wealth all his life. His problem was that he did not open the Bible that contained all his wealth. It is only those who go deep into the depths in Christ who discover their riches. Those who go further in Christ discover the sweeter things.

In all relationships, the deeper you go, the more you discover the person. Those who go for superficial touches never get to the wealth of any relationship. No wonder, they complain that they do not have friends. Some people are like butterflies. They touch everyone superficially and then complain about everyone. They have no time to plunge into any relationship.

CHOSEN BEFORE THE FOUNDATION OF THE WORLD

*I*n Ephesians 1:4 we read,

Even as he chose us in him before the foundation of the world, that we should be holy and blameless before him."

God did something in Christ before the foundation of the world. How old are you? Or better still, how old is the earth? Geologists tell us that the earth is about 4.5 billion years old. But you were formed in Christ before the foundation of the earth. Therefore, in Christ, you are more than 4.5 billion years old. If you are one of those who fear ageing, then you are already very old. Imagine for how long you have been in Christ?

You were elected before the foundation of the world. You did not elect yourself. If you were to elect yourself, it could only have been to hell. That is where personal merit, good works and righteousness lead to. You could only elect yourself unto eternal damnation. But in Christ, you have been elected unto eternal salvation.

The great mystery I want to share with you is that even before the foundation of the world, God chose you. You are of the utmost importance. You are not just something that was done in a hurry. You are not nature's error. If you are in Christ, you are not in this world by accident.

There is a brother who said to me, "Brother Zach., I almost never existed. My parents had me as an afterthought. They had already had eight children, stopped and went for about ten years, and behold, I came forth." He is a dear brother in the Lord. I told him, "You are not an afterthought. Before the foundation of the world, God put you in Christ. You are a very important person."

Do you see the value that God places on you? You are of such precious worth to His heart that before the foundation of the world, He had put you in Christ. We read that we are the elect of God – and indeed we are. Do you know that you are an elect of God? It is wonderful that you responded to the love of God. But before you responded, you were already chosen in Him. Do you see how solid your foundation is? It does not just depend on the decision you made.

Though this decision is very important, something greater than it was at the back of it – you were chosen by God, and placed in Christ. Do you know for how long God has put you in Christ? For at least 4.5 billion years! God has been taking care of you in Christ for that long. I do not know how many years are left before the second coming of Jesus, but I have this firm assurance, that the One who has kept us in Him for 4.5 billion years, will keep us for the few years and days left before Christ comes for us. I do not fear the future.

If He was faithful for more than 4.5 billion years, what is one hundred years or more, for as long as He tarries? He will be faithful. Be fully assured that He will be faithful. The One who has chosen you in Him will perfect that which He began. Some people think that they are in Christ today, only to be out tomorrow. Christ does not have a list of the elect today, and tomorrow another one that omits your name. That is not how God works. Your name has been on His list for over 4.5 billion years.

Irrespective of the warring of the devil – right from heaven, when he wanted to take the throne of God, or in the garden of Eden, and all the other wars he has fought to take over power, God has won and kept you in Christ. The One who has won all the battles of the years past, will again win all the future battles, and present you without spot, blemish or wrinkle.

5

HOLY AND BLAMELESS

*H*e chose us in Christ, not so that we should be saved and that the others should perish. That is not of God. He saved us so that we should be holy and blameless before Him. We have been chosen for holiness and blamelessness. The predestination grace of God has holiness and blamelessness before God as its purpose. God chose us and placed us in Christ for this one purpose; holiness and blamelessness.

If we do not separate ourselves radically from sin and unto Him, then we have set out to fight against His eternal purpose. This is a serious issue. For over 4.5 billion years, God has been working on our behalf with the one purpose of holiness and blamelessness in mind. Will it not be madness, if for the few years that we have left, before the trumpet sounds for us to be taken to be with Jesus, that we should give ourselves to the practice of sin and thereby frustrate His purpose?

I have been chosen to be holy, separated from the world and unto Him. In the light of what God has done over the last 4.5 billion years, I am compelled to be holy. I am condemned unto holiness. No one has any right to practise sin, even in the smallest thing. This is because by doing so, he sets himself against what God has been doing for more than 4.5 billon years.

If you love the world, its glory and its things, you compromise the demands of God. If you live only for this passing world, you have missed it all. If you build a nation for one hundred years and someone comes along by a Coup d'Etat to destroy it, how will you take it? Think of a woman who has spent two hours cooking; then her child comes and pours down all the contents of her pot – the child will be sure to receive a good lashing. What do you think God will do to you if you dare try to waste His over 4.5 billion years of work? In addition to it, you have cost Him His dear Son!

With this in mind, how can we then practice sin in any form? It will be like scattering and destroying what God has been doing for more than 4.5 billion years. It will be piercing the heart of God. Once a mother said, "I spent my life working for this child, but he has broken my heart." Sinning is breaking God's heart. When God considers what he has invested in you and the blood of the Lamb shed at Calvary, He must be heart-broken at the slightest sin you commit.

What sin is still there in your life? What is causing you that restlessness that has taken away the peace of God from your heart? What is at the root of the fact that you have lost the way of true joy? Are you satisfied? Have you pierced God's heart with a knife and pushed it in by your sin? Could it be that after God has worked for so many years, the world should so capture your heart that you are very busy trying to gain it, that you have lost that intimacy with God, that perfect satisfaction that you once knew?

Before, you saw things clearly, but now, everything is getting blurred. Before, your priorities were clear, but now you have lost the sense of a clear direction. The Lord does not fully satisfy you anymore; you think the world will. Of course, it will not!

There must be radical separation from sin and from the love of the world, and radical consecration to God's purposes, without which our election is meaningless. Where there is a divided heart, there is war against the electing act of God. Is yours a divided heart? Do something about it today.

Christ Himself is holy and blameless. We were therefore chosen and put in the holy and blameless One. In this election, God set out to produce a people for Himself, who are holy and blameless. Our holiness and blamelessness must be at the level that can stand before God. Personally, it does not consist in comparing my holiness with the holiness of some other person in Christ or in the world. My holiness must meet the level of divine approval. I can no longer be satisfied that I have stopped doing the things I used to do in the world. The question is, "Does my holiness meet His approval? Does my blamelessness meet His approval?"

It must be holiness in heart, not simply in my acts. What I am must be approved before God. It has nothing to do with sounding a trumpet that my heart is not divided. It should be such that when God looks at my heart, He testifies that it satisfies Him.

Take away some minutes from this reading and wait a moment before God, and let the Holy Spirit say something to you about the condition of your heart. This is of utmost importance, as it is invariably tied to your eternal election. Write down what you already know is wrong with your heart, and what God tells you about the condition of your heart. Maybe the Holy Spirit has been talking to you about this for a long time. Now is the time to do something about it.

The apostle Paul says,

> *But by the grace of God I am what I am, and his grace toward me was not in vain. On the contrary, I worked harder than any of them, though it was not I, but the grace of God which is with me* (1 Corinthians 15:10).

Make sure that God's election of you is not in vain. Live your life everyday before God. Do not try to paint an image that is not the truth about you. There is no need to pretend. Expose yourself to Him twenty-four hours a day. Live with the knowledge that He is seeing you, as indeed He is.

LIKE CHRIST

We have read that,

He destined us in love to be his sons through Jesus Christ, according to the purpose of his will, to the praise of his glorious grace which he freely bestowed on us in the Beloved (Ephesians 1:5-6).

Christ is the Beloved One of God. It is in Him that God bestowed His grace on us. Love, not merit, is at the basis of our election. We were destined to be sons like Jesus Christ.

Sonship here does not have to do with gender. It is not the opposite of being a daughter. It talks of maturity in Christ. We are to attain maturity in Christ and be as mature as Christ. It is in the purpose of God that the adopted sons should be like the Beloved. There must be the closest resemblance possible between the Begotten Son and the adopted sons. Jesus is the Beloved Son and we are the adopted sons. God's heart is gladdened when the adopted sons become like the Begotten Son.

AN OVERCOMER LOT

*T*he Bible says,

...When he appears we shall be like him... (1 John 3:2).

That moment will be a moment of joy for the Father. At that time, there will be no difference between the "Beloved" and the adopted sons. That is why God is anxious for the overcomers.

Overcomers are those who, before the coming of the Lord, mature in holiness, in blamelessness and in total separation from the world unto Him. These should be mature in total consecration to His purposes before His coming. These ones press on to become the first fruit that satisfies the heart of God.

The overcomers have a special place and prize before God. They give God the privilege of having a foretaste of the age to come, when there will be no difference between the Beloved and the adopted sons. The question is, "Will there be some to pay that price of total abandonment and total consecration to the point of being misunderstood, but to the satisfaction of God's heart, thereby winning a place in His heart that others may not attain?"

There is an opportunity today, to stretch out with God, unto the fullness of Christ, in a life of total abandonment to Him in everything, and thereby establish a gap between you and the rest that will never,

never be bridged. Those who step out now in this manner, will win a place in God's heart that others will never be able to win.

Even with human beings, you know that the first love of a man's heart is always very special. Those who step ahead, will occupy such a special place in God's heart that others will never attain. The sad thing is that, faced with the possibility of winning a special place in the heart of God, many allow one thing or another to stand in their way. For the person who is still level-headed and who can see, there is no substitute to radical abandonment to God now.

Do we want to give God the first fruit of those who will be like Christ, before the coming age? If we do not give Him that first fruit, we will be the losers.

CHAPTER TWO

In him we have redemption through his blood, the forgiveness of our trespasses, according to the riches of his grace which he lavished upon us. For he has made known to us in all wisdom and insight the mystery of his will, according to his purpose which he set forth in Christ as a plan for the fullness of time, to unite all things in him, things in heaven and things on earth. In him, according to the purpose of him who accomplishes all things according to the counsel of his will, we who first hoped in Christ have been destined and appointed to live for the praise of his glory. In him you also, who have heard the word of truth, the gospel of your salvation, and have believed in him, were sealed with the promised Holy Spirit, which is the guarantee of our inheritance until we acquire possession of it, to the praise of his glory.

— *EPHESIANS 1: 7-14*

REDEMPTION THROUGH HIS BLOOD

*T*he passage above states that,

In him we have redemption through his blood, the forgiveness of our trespasses, according to the riches of his grace which he lavished upon us.

In Him we are both redeemed and forgiven. We are the redeemed of God. Our redemption and forgiveness are through His blood.

When you meet demon-possessed people, you find that they resist both the name and the blood of the Lord Jesus Christ. The devil does not want you to mention the blood of Jesus. Modernists who want to distort the power of the word of God do not want to talk about the blood of Jesus Christ. I was reading of a Reverend Pastor who for twenty-four years, did not want to hear anything about the blood of Jesus Christ. That was before he was converted to Christ. He said, "Somehow, the blood of the Lord Jesus did not please me."

The devil does not love the blood of the Lamb. His agents do not love the blood of the Lamb. That is why when you talk about the blood of Jesus, they take offence. This is because the blood is the instrument which God used for our redemption and forgiveness.

If you take away the blood, there is no redemption and no forgiveness of sins. In Egypt, salvation for the Israelites was dependent on the blood. God had said,

> *The blood shall be a sign for you, upon the houses where you are; and when I see the blood, I will pass over you, and no plague shall fall upon you to destroy you, when I smite the land of Egypt* (Exodus 12:13).

Wherever there is the blood, there is no judgment and no condemnation. Through His blood, we have been redeemed and forgiven.

Do not keep your sins anymore. The blood has been shed. The Bible says,

> *There no longer remains a sacrifice for sins* (Hebrews 10:26).

The blood has already been shed. Do you know it? If you do, what is your attitude to the sin you have already confessed? Do you remain miserable after you have repented of it? Are you of the doctrine that when you have been forgiven you come out of the sin slowly? No! That is wrong. You rather praise God and continue as if you have never sinned. Your sin has been laid on Christ and you bear it no more. You are covered with the blood of the Lamb. God cannot condemn you for blood-covered sin. There are things which God cannot do - He cannot jump over the blood of Christ to punish anyone, irrespective of the heat of His anger against that person.

THE RICHES OF HIS GRACE

*T*he redemption and forgiveness of God are,

According to the riches of his grace which he lavished upon us
(Ephesians 1:7).

Grace means that we do not merit it. It also means that there are no limits to the dimensions. Notice that it is not only according to His grace, but according to the riches of His grace. Grace could be expressed thus:

God's
Riches
At
Christ's
Expense.

God treats us according to the riches of His grace. Furthermore, He does not give us this grace stingily - He lavishes it. Yes, – He lavishes it!

This reminds me of a brother who came to ask me about tithes. He thought that giving ten percent of his income to God was too much, and was looking for ways of reducing it. He came to ask me whether the ten percent was calculated before the salary has been taxed or after the taxes have been calculated and deducted. When I asked him where the problem was, he told me that the difference was considerable. He was concerned lest by error he gave God more. When God gives to us, He does not think like this brother. He lavishes.

The other problem is with the way we give love to others. Often, we are afraid lest we give people too much of it. We want to check the warmth. But God is not like that. If He were like that, life would be too difficult for us. He gives in lavishing measures. He gives as though he would empty heaven.

Let me take an example from the depth and extent to which He forgives us. How many times have you gone to Him for His pardon? Has He ever sent you back? Have you ever thought of not going to Him for forgiveness again because you have been there for the same sin or another which you have committed again? Did you ever think of perishing in your sin because you think that God's well of forgiveness might have dried up? That would be wrong, and you would go to hell. As many times as we sin, we take our sin to Him. If it requires going to Him one million times, none who goes there has ever been sent back.[1]

Those of us who do counselling know that when someone has come and truly confessed his failures deeply, without hiding things, without pretending, you cannot help but love that person. It is the very opposite of what should be expected at the natural level. Somehow, the Holy Spirit of God flows to the person who is down on his knees, in deep repentance, to lift him up. When he comes, confessing his need of the blood, of grace, then that grace is abundantly lavished upon him. But when someone is pretending, there is an obstacle. God has no use for pretenders.

When did you last experience the abundance of His grace lavished on you? When did you last go to seek for it in deep repentance? Have you committed the sin you thought was the unpardonable sin? Take it to the cross and see whether it is stronger than the blood. The hymn writer says:

There is a fountain filled with blood
Drawn from Emmanuel's veins.

And sinners, plunged beneath that blood,
Lose all their guilty stains.

It is just like God to lavish; to give without measure. Yes, we have often sung of Jesus Christ as the gift of God without measure, the One with whom we shall reign together.

Look at those of us who want to reign with Him - we deserve the worst. It is utterly miraculous that sinners, who deserve the worst from God, should one day reign in total holiness with the Son of God. God is a miraculous person. Glory be to His holy name!

THE MYSTERY OF HIS WILL

*I*n Ephesians 1:9 we read that,

For he has made known to us in all wisdom and insight the mystery of his will, according to his purpose which he set forth in Christ as a plan for the fullness of time, to unite all things in him, things in heaven and things on earth.

We know God's will. Do not say that you do not know it. What is that will? His will is that we might be like Jesus Christ. As simple as that. We do not need books on philosophy to know His will. If you are like Jesus, you have done God's will. If you do what Jesus would do in every situation, you have done God's will.

His will is a mystery, because Jesus Himself is a mystery. His will, which He makes known to us, concerns His purposes set forth in Christ. God's will has not been set forth in science, in cosmology or in the other sciences. It has not been set forth in techniques and instruments. It has been set forth in a person, in the Lord Jesus. Since Christ is in us, we have God's will resident in us. We have God's purpose and His goal resident in us.

ALL THINGS HAVE BEEN UNITED IN CHRIST

*O*ften, and in error, we try to grasp teachings coming from left and right. God has summed up all things in Jesus Christ, and has given Him to us. Jesus Christ has been made our salvation and God's purpose for us. When you have Christ, you have God's purpose in you. Stop looking left and right. Look into yourself, into the resident Christ. It is such folly to go looking left and right trying to use the methods of the world. God's purpose and methods are set forth in Christ.

God is seeking, to unite all things in him - things in heaven and things on earth. By granting that all things find themselves in Christ, God is seeking to unite everything in Him. Anything that is not in Christ has missed God's purpose. God therefore begins by giving us Jesus.

That which God has done in us, He wants to do it for all creation. He wants to unite all creation in Christ. In Colossians 1:17 we read,

He is before all things, and in him all things hold together.

Without Him, all things fall into bits. Any life and family that are in Christ hold together. They hold together that they might come to fullness in Him. All that is in Him is totally integrated. In the Millennial Kingdom when Christ will be Lord and ruler of the whole earth, when all things shall be fully related to Him, there shall be total harmony. If there is discord anywhere, it is evident that things are not rightly related to Him. We should ensure that our lives are totally and rightly related to Him.

This means that every other religion in which Christ is not central is in chaos. Things do not hold together for those who are held captive in those religions. Things hold together only in Christ. God unites only in Christ.

People want to unite things in their country, continent, race or language and so on, outside of Christ. By whatever worldly standard, things do not hold together outside of Christ. All human Systems fall into bits outside of Christ. In Christ Jesus, everything holds together.

Is there some area of your life that is not holding together? Where is there no peace, no harmony in your life? Surrender to the Lord Jesus Christ and things shall hold together. Is it well in your home? If not, surrender to Jesus and all things shall hold together. We must do everything mindful of God's purpose to unite all things together in Christ.

THE COUNSEL OF HIS WILL

*W*e have read that God *accomplishes all things according to the counsel of his will.*

He is completely sovereign. He consults no one. There are many believers who, instead of praying, try to advice God. God only works according to His perfect will. According to the counsel of His will,

> *We who first hoped in Christ have been destined and appointed to live for the praise of his glory.*

We have been destined and appointed to live for the praise of His glory. That is the wonder about being in Christ. We have been appointed. The predestination has been followed by the appointment. We are actually, now living for the praise of His glory. It is not a thing for the future. It is here and it is now.

Every believer has been predestined to live for the glory of God. To Jeremiah God said,

> *Before I formed you in the womb I knew you, and before you were born I consecrated you; I appointed you a prophet to the nations* (Jeremiah 1:5).

You too have been given your job and an office. You are a servant of the King of heaven, an ambassador of Christ.

You are an ambassador of heaven to your family, neighbourhood, tribe, nation, wherever you are. You are not just anybody. When you walk, do so with the importance and dignity of an ambassador. You must also know that if there is trouble, you have to phone home. The lines of heaven are never jammed.

If you need to be taken out of the place where you are ambassador, you will be whisked off in a matter of seconds. Are you proud of your country? If you are, then you cannot be jealous of the country where you have been sent. In any case, the cheapest thing in your own country is gold. The streets are made of gold. The dust of heaven is gold. May God open our eyes to see this.

We have been appointed to live for the praise of His glory. We are to live in such a way that when we are seen, He should be glorified. When people live solely for the Lord, there is more worship for Him in heaven. Angels will rejoice when a saint walks in integrity and in the fullness of the Lord Jesus. They rejoice by falling before the Lord and worshipping Him.

Even on earth, among the saints, when they see a life consecrated to God, they praise God for such a believer. When they see a life totally yielded to God, they are challenged to do the same. In this way, the more people are totally yielded to Christ, the more praise goes up to the Father.

Are you provoked by the lives of others? Recently I saw how some believer was giving to the Lord and I was provoked to give more. My prayer is that our lives would provoke each other to good works. Let us labour to ensure that as others see us make progress, they too may be provoked to make progress, so that there will be more praise to the glory of His name.

13

SEALED WITH THE HOLY SPIRIT

We have read that,

In him you also, who have heard the word of truth, the gospel of your salvation, and have believed in him, were sealed with the promised Holy Spirit, which is the guarantee of our inheritance until we acquire possession of it, to the praise of his glory.

Immediately a person believes in the Lord Jesus Christ, the Lord seals him with the Holy Spirit. A seal is a stamp of ownership. We are sealed with the Holy Spirit as God's stamp of ownership.

Once, Jesus was preaching and someone asked Him whether taxes ought to be paid to Caesar or not. He took a coin and asked them whose inscription it was. They said it was Caesar's. Then He said to them,

Render therefore to Caesar the things that are Caesar's, and to God the things that are God's (Matthew 22:21).

Caesar's seal on the coin made the coin his. In the same manner, God's seal of the Holy Spirit on you makes you His.

It is God's intention that when men see you, because of the evidence of the Holy Spirit He has put in you, they will say, "Give this one to

Jesus." The Holy Spirit in us is God's mark of ownership that says, "This one is Mine."

Dear saint, do you know to whom you belong? You belong to God. Stop running away from Him. There is His stamp of ownership on you; the Holy Spirit.

God has put His Holy Spirit in the totality of your being. Every part of your body belongs to Him. Everything in you belongs to Him. You are not only an ambassador for Christ. You belong to Him. You are His. You are God's property. Every inch of you spells His ownership of you.

The other aspect of being sealed with the Holy Spirit has to do with security. The Holy Spirit is, as it were, a lock to a box as it were, into which Christ has put you. You can consider the Holy Spirit as both the box and the lock. When you believe, God takes you, puts you in the Holy Spirit, locks you up in Him, puts the key in His pocket and goes away. The devil can come and knock and knock and knock to no avail. The treasure inside the box remains safe and secure. In the fullness of time, the Master will come with His key, open it, and find His treasure, secure. The devil cannot damage it. All of hell cannot damage the treasure.

Our security and assurance are in the Holy Spirit. God has indeed put us into the Holy Spirit, and who can kick against Him? Take some funny story I got – Someone said, "Let us arrest the Holy Spirit because He is causing a lot of confusion." I wish him success. No one can stop the Holy Spirit. He must have His way. Our security is guaranteed.

Let me insist that the Holy Spirit will have His way. He will have His way in your life. Stop wasting time in rebellion. Do you not see that you are only wasting time? He will win. You are going to do what He wants you to do! You are going to go where He wants you to go. You are going to give Him your whole life, completely. Your property is going to belong to Him. Do you think He is going to begin losing battles with you? Never! He has always won His battles. He is only giving you some time. Do not think that you are winning. Never mind. He will win!

There are those plans of yours where you have kept Him out. Never mind, you will not go far with them. You are going to follow His own plans. When He intervenes, you will look for your own plans and not find them. Stop making plans that will soon be gone. Why waste time? Those who have cats know that sometimes a powerful cat catches a rat and begins to play with it. It will free it a little, let it be and the rat may think that it has had its freedom. But just as it tries to run away, a single skip from the cat says the rat was mistaken.

Stop trying to resist the Holy Spirit. Do not pretend. You will ultimately surrender. You cannot be happy away from Him. You cannot cause a coup d'Etat against His will concerning you. You will fail, and He will win.

The Winner, the Holy Spirit, is the Guarantor that we shall enter into our full inheritance. He is also the Guarantor that God will have His inheritance in us. He is a two-fold guarantor. He guarantees that we shall have all that is ours in Christ and He guarantees that God will have all that is His in us, to the praise of His glory.

CHAPTER THREE

For this reason, because I have heard of your faith in the Lord Jesus and your love towards all saints, I do not cease to give thanks for you, remembering you in my prayers, that the God of our Lord Jesus Christ, the Father of glory, may give you a spirit of wisdom and of revelation in the knowledge of him, having the eyes of your heart enlightened, that you may know what is the hope to which he has called you, what are the riches of his glorious inheritance in the saints, and what is the immeasurable greatness of his power in us who believe, according to the working of his great might which he accomplished in Christ when he raised him from the dead and made him sit at his right hand in the heavenly places, far above all rule and authority and power and dominion, and above every name that is named, not only in this age but also that which is to come; and he has put all things under his feet and has made him the head over all things for the church, which is his body, the fullness of him who fills all in all.

— EPHESIANS 1:15-23

And you he made alive, when you were dead through the trespasses and sins in which you once walked, following the course of this world, following the prince of the power of the air, the spirit that is now at work in the sons of disobedience. Among these we all once lived in the passions of our flesh, following the desires of the body and mind, and so we were by nature children of wrath, like the rest of mankind. But God, who is rich in mercy, out of the great love with which he loved us, even when we were dead through our trespasses, made us alive together with Christ (by grace you have been saved), and raised up with him, and made us sit with him in the heavenly places in Christ Jesus, that in the coming ages he might show the immeasurable riches of his grace in kindness toward us in Christ Jesus ...

For by grace you have been saved through faith; and this is not your own doing, it is the gift of God – not because of works, least any man should boast. For we are his workmanship, created in Christ Jesus for good works, which God prepared beforehand, that we should walk in them.

— EPHESIANS 2:1-6, 8-10

REPENTANCE TOWARDS GOD AND FAITH IN THE LORD JESUS

*W*e have seen our glorious position in Christ. We have seen the fact that we have been sealed in Him; as a source of protection and as a mark of ownership. We are such a privileged people. As the apostle sees all these things accomplished in Christ, he says,

> *For this reason, because I have heard of your faith in the Lord Jesus,*
> *and your love towards all saints, I do not cease to give thanks for*
> *you, remembering you in my prayers* (Ephesians 1:15-16).

Before conversion, these Ephesians had to repent toward God, and put their faith in the Lord Jesus Christ. For salvation, there must be repentance toward God and faith in the Lord Jesus Christ. This is the experience of all who come to the Lord Jesus Christ.

When they have come to the Lord Jesus Christ, what are they to be taught? They are now to hear of faith in the Lord Jesus Christ. Their faith in Him has to grow and deepen. They must also love all the saints. We may put it as below:

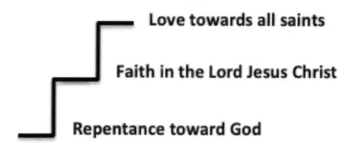

15

LOVE TOWARDS ALL SAINTS - 1

hen I come to Christ, it is no longer enough for me just to have faith in the Lord Jesus Christ. I must go on and love all the saints. We are all called to love all the saints. All who have repented toward God and have faith in the Lord Jesus Christ are concerned. They may be mature or immature. They may see all the counsel of God or not. They may be black or white. They may differ with you over one or more issues. Whatever the case, provided they have repented toward God and have faith in the Lord Jesus, you owe them love. There is no choice about this matter.

We have been commanded to love all the brethren. God expects it of us. Someone may have repented towards God, has faith in the Lord Jesus Christ, but is clumsy in character - you are to love him still. He may not understand very many things - you are to love him still. You owe love to all who have repented toward God and have faith in the Lord Jesus Christ.

We are to love all the saints as Christ loved us. He loved us when we were still sinners. It was not when we were pleasing to Him. The Bible says,

> *While we were still weak, at the right time Christ died for the ungodly. Why, one will hardly die for a righteous man—though perhaps for a good man one will dare even to die. But God shows*

his love for us in that while we were yet sinners Christ died for us
(Romans 5:6-8).

In the same way, even when the other believers do not yet see what we have seen, and have not entered into the experiences God has led us into, we ought to love them. Even when they are immature saints, we are to love them. May we pay our debt of love to all the saints.

Begin by loving those in your house. Some people want to go and love those who are a thousand miles away, when they have not loved the people in their own house. If there is a brother or sister in your house whom you do not love, then you have failed. Husbands, begin by loving your wives, and vice versa. Husbands and wives should love their children and children should love their parents. If you do not love the relative you are housing, you have failed God.

This love must continue to include the people in your immediate fellowship. You cannot love the brethren in another assembly, without being able to love those of your own fellowship. If there is someone nearby, begin by loving him or her. Our responsibility is to love, not to condemn.

Paul takes it for granted that loving all the saints will be the normal attitude toward all those who are in the Kingdom. If we do not love all the saints, we are abnormal. Some people would rather sell all they have and give the money to the poor, than love all the saints. Paul says,

If I speak in the tongues of men and of angels, but have not love, I am a noisy gong or a clanging cymbal. And if I have prophetic powers, and understand all the mysteries and all knowledge, and if I have all faith, so as to remove mountains, but have not love, I am nothing. If I give away all I have, and if I deliver my body to be burned, but have not love, I gain nothing (1 Corinthians 13:1-3).

LOVE TOWARDS ALL SAINTS - 2

*I*t was not miracles that worked salvation's plan. It was love. In the ministry of the Lord, great miracles came into play. But the heart of it all was love—God's love.

Let us once more bear in mind that if we fail in love, we have indeed failed. Failure in love is eliminatory. If we fail in love, we fail in discipleship; we cannot be disciples; we have opted out of discipleship.

If you make yourself inaccessible to love, you have equally failed. Some people carry their cages and move about in them for fear that someone may reach out to them in love. It was said of the early church, – "See how these people love one another." The early church had many weaknesses, nonetheless, they scored highly in love. In our day, we seem to specialise in scoring high in correct doctrine. I am not in for wrong doctrine anyway. But what is the use of loveless correct doctrine? God laid a foundation of love and built with the right doctrine around this love. May we be like Him.

It may be very easy to say, "I love God," but sometimes it is difficult to prove it. However, if I do not love my brother nearby, it becomes obvious. Let us prove that we love God by loving the brethren. If not, we are hypocrites.

PRAYING FOR THE SAINTS

*P*aul's prayer for the saints was, that

> *the God of our Lord Jesus Christ, the Father of glory, may give you a Spirit of wisdom and of revelation in the knowledge of him, having the eyes of your heart enlightened, that you may know what is the hope to which he has called you, what are the riches of his glorious inheritance in the saints, and what is the immeasurable greatness of his power in us who believe* (Ephesians 1:17-19).

The Spirit of wisdom and of revelation, which Paul prayed that the brethren should have was to be evidenced in a three-fold manifestation in them:

- Knowledge of the hope to which God has called them.
- Knowledge of the riches of His glorious inheritance in the saints and
- Knowledge of the immeasurable greatness of His power in them.

THE HOPE OF OUR CALLING IN CHRIST

The hope to which God has called us is that we might be like Christ in character and in ministry. It is neither only in character nor only in ministry; the problem is that we try to separate the two. That is not God's purpose. The purpose of God is that we put on the character of Christ, and also serve as Christ served, with the same dedication, boldness and power.

Some people only focus on Christian character and others focus on power for service. No one should be contented with anything less than the fullness of the character of Christ and of the power of the Lord. None should be contented with the power of the Lord when it is not backed by the character of the Lord. We are to make progress in the school of character formation and in the school of spiritual power.

It is also in the purpose of God that the church might function with all the spiritual gifts, and that the world might be taken by the horns in the power of the Lord. We must reject mediocrity. Our inheritance in Christ is both in the character and power of the Lord. We have to know this, without which we may not enter into them. You cannot enter into that which you do not know about. God has said,

My people are destroyed for lack of knowledge (Hosea 4:6).

It is of utmost importance that the eyes of our hearts may be enlightened. Our hearts have eyes. It is something beyond the natural mind. It goes beyond the physical dimension. It is in the realm of revelation and experience. As one makes progress into Christ, the eyes of his heart become enlightened.

On the other hand, as one plunges himself into sin, he progressively plunges into darkness. With such darkness, one finds that the Lord no longer talks to him by revelations, dreams, His word, ... Sin darkens the eyes of the heart, whereas holiness opens the eyes of the heart. That is why it is inconceivable that a believer should remain in sin, however small the sin may be.

You do not need a large object before the eyes are shut away from light. The tiniest thing in your eyes makes you unable to see. That is what the smallest sin does to the eyes of the heart. It takes just a tiny bit of sin in your eyes and you can see no more. There must, therefore, be no joking even with what people call small sins. In the eyes of the heart, the smallest sin has tragic consequences in the spiritual. The smallest sin is terribly dangerous. Those who walk in holiness have their eyes enlightened in an increasing measure.

Have you made Christ-likeness in character and in service your goal? God expects you to know, and to make it your goal. If not, you will go nowhere. Do not be too lazy to establish goals in this domain.

19

THE RICHES OF HIS GLORIOUS INHERITANCE IN THE SAINTS -1

*H*ow rich is the believer? He has been blessed with every spiritual blessing in the heavenly places in Christ Jesus. This said, it remains our task to make that which has been given, to fully become ours in experience. There is no spiritual blessing in the heavenly places that has not been given to us in Christ Jesus.

All of the Promised Land was given to the children of Israel and they were to possess all of it. If they would not rise up to possess it, they would not have it. It had been given to them, all of it, nothing was held back, but they were to enter and make it theirs. If you do not appropriate what has been given to you, you will live as if you had nothing.

Very many believers are too lazy to enter into their inheritance. Have you too settled for something less than your full inheritance? May we not be lacking in the faith that it takes to enter into our full inheritance. Our inheritance is holiness; no sin. We are to be without sin. We are to be perfect, for He is perfect. But then, many of us are settling for something less than perfection. God has given us perfection, and calls us into it. In the following verses, the Bible demands, nay, commands perfection:

- *You, therefore, must be perfect, as your heavenly Father is perfect* (Matthew 5:48).

- *Jesus said to him, 'If you would be perfect, go, sell what you possess and give to the poor, and you will have treasure in heaven; and come, follow me'* (Matthew 19:21).
- *Finally, brethren, farewell. Be perfect, be of good comfort, be of one mind, live in peace; and the God of love and peace shall be with you* (2 Corinthians 13:11, KJV).
- *Let us therefore, as many as be perfect, be thus minded: and if in anything ye be otherwise minded, God shall reveal even this unto you* (Philippians 3:15, KJV).
- *That the man of God may be perfect, thoroughly furnished unto all good works* (2 Timothy 3:17, KJV).
- *And let steadfastness have its full effect, that you may be perfect and complete, lacking nothing* (James 1:4).

20

THE RICHES OF HIS GLORIOUS INHERITANCE IN THE SAINTS - 2

We have been blessed with every spiritual gift in the heavenly places, and God wants us to enter into them. We have been given:

- **Perfect health** – we must enter into it.
- **Perfect holiness** – we must enter into it.
- **Authority over principalities and powers** – we must enter into it and more.

If we do not enter into all of these, they shall not be our experience.

When God gave Abraham the whole land of Canaan, He told him to arise and walk across the length of it. Wherever he set his feet would become his. Wherever he set his feet, it was his. God gave him all, but he had to set foot on it, own it and possess it for himself. Where he did not set foot on, he did not possess.

The greatest sin of the church is that she has failed, through unbelief, to enter into all that God has for her. The greatest sin I have committed is the sin of unbelief. But I have repented of it. May our eyes be opened to God's glorious inheritance in us, the saints. Jesus Christ is in us as the hope of glory. The glorious inheritance is right in us. It is not outside - Christ in us, the hope of glory.

As you enter into the fullness of Christ, you enter into the fullness of your inheritance. He is in you. Believe God and enter into your inheritance. If you believe that you were made to sin and perish, it will happen. I am very worried about some people who say, "I will not evangelise until I become holy. I am still sanctifying myself." The problem is that they have been sanctifying themselves for the last one month, six months, one year, two years, five years. They have been caught in the trap of the devil, so that they are kept out of the glorious inheritance of the saints in Christ Jesus. You can enter into your full inheritance of the sanctified life by an act of faith. Jesus Christ has been made unto us our sanctification. You do not need to spend years learning to be sanctified. You will never learn it. Simply enter into the experience, by faith.

Believe God and enter into your glorious inheritance. He has given you all that you need. How long does it take to believe God? That is how long it takes to enter into sanctification. It takes that same length of time to enter into God's power, victory and into all that God has in store for us. It takes faith - and the Bible says,

Without faith it is impossible to please God (Hebrew 11:12).

For example, God has told us that the devil has been conquered. We may choose to believe it, or look around for the noise the devil is making and doubt everything.

The other tragedy is that we believe our experiences instead of believing God.

We are not to accept limitations. The only power that the devil has is the power that we let him have. God disarmed principalities and powers and made a public show of them, triumphing over them by His glorious cross. Do we believe it? Are we believing-atheists? May we not continue to stand in God's way through unbelief.

Faith sees it, grasps it, seizes it and owns it now. Faith believes and confesses what God has done, now. We walk by faith and not by sight. It is to this that we are called. He has given us everything. Shall we continue in poverty and sin, allowing the devil to lead us into more sin so that we confess it? When shall we begin to confess victory? Everything is possible to the one who believes. Those who believe confess the word, because God has raised the word above His own name.

There is a sense in which God's name can fail, but His word can never fail. He has placed His word higher than His name. I was asking myself, "Have I been bewitched? Have we been bewitched? How come we read clear statements about what God has done, of what we are and not enter into the experience they inform us about?" If someone told you, "This is your food, eat it." What do you do? You may say, "I am not qualified. Even those who are better than I do not eat this food. I will first go and think about it." This is how we have behaved and lost the great things God has in store for us.

21

THE IMMEASURABLE GREATNESS OF HIS POWER IN THE SAINTS

*W*e are rich, immeasurably rich. There is nothing that was in Christ that God has not put into us. God has put into you all that was in Christ. That is why the scriptures talk of the immeasurable greatness of His power in us who believe. It is greatness without measure, in us, put there by God. The power of God in us, in you, is immeasurably great. The greatest atomic power of heaven has been placed in you.

The breath, length, height and depth of God's power in you are beyond measure. That power is not hidden in a cave somewhere. It is in us, in you. The power is not outside of us. It is not only in the leaders. It is in all who believe. It is in all of us who have repented toward God and have faith in the Lord Jesus Christ. The totality of the power of God; Father, Son and Holy Spirit has been put into you, according to the working of His great might.

It was a very great event, when God put His great power in us. It required great power, the working of His great might. It was not a simple event. The installation was tremendously successful. The power of God; Father, Son and Holy Spirit is operative in us who believe. O God, open our eyes to see it!

It is that same power that was operative in Christ when God raised Him from the dead, and made Him to sit in the heavenly places, far above all rule and authority and power and dominion and every name that is named, not only in this age, but also in the age to come. And He has put all things under His feet and made Him the head of all things.

Look at Jesus Christ; dead on the cross, made alive by God, then raised and seated in the heavenly places. We could present it as follows:

> **Jesus Christ:** Seated in the heavenly places, above all rule, authority, power, dominion, all names that can be named.
>
> **Jesus Christ:** Raised from the dead
>
> **Jesus Christ:** Dead on the cross and buried

Everything has been put under the feet of Christ, and He has been made the Head of all things. Christ is seated in such a way that every other thing is under His feet.

Let us now turn to the believer. He was dead in his trespasses and sins. He followed the prince of this world, the devil. The prince of the world is the spirit that is now at work in the sons of disobedience. The Bible says,

> *Among these we all once lived in the passions of our flesh, following the desires of the body and mind, and so we were by nature children of wrath, like the rest of mankind* (Ephesians 2:3).

We all, everybody, went one hundred percent off. But God, rich in mercy, out of the great love He had for us, even while we were dead in our trespasses, made us alive with Christ. He lifted us up, together with Christ, united with Him. We were put in Him so that we may have one destiny with Christ. The destiny of Christ has become our destiny. The glory of Christ has become our glory. The victory of Christ has become our victory.

We are no longer dead in our trespasses and sins. We have come to life together with Christ, by grace. He raised us up with Him, and made us sit with Him in heavenly places. That is where you are! Can

Christ be on the throne and then you are not there? Impossible! Where He is, there we are, there you are!

This is the glorious implication of being in Christ. That is what it means to have died with Him and to have been raised with Him. That is what it means to be a Christian. In the coming ages, He will show the immeasurable riches, of His grace and kindness to us. The world does not know what we are, but the day is coming when the sons of God shall be revealed.

CHAPTER FOUR

And he has put all things under his feet and has made him the head over all things for the church, which is his body, the fullness of him who fills all in all.

— EPHESIANS 1:22-23

For this reason I, Paul, a prisoner for Christ Jesus on behalf of you Gentiles - assuming that you have heard of the stewardship of God's grace that was given to me for you, how the mystery was made known to me by revelation, as I have written briefly. When you read this you can perceive my insight into the mystery of Christ, which was not made known to the sons of men in other generations as it has been revealed to his holy apostles and prophets by the Spirit; that is, how the Gentiles are fellow heirs, members of the same body, and partakers of the promise in Christ Jesus through the gospel.

Of this gospel I was made a minister according to the gift of God's grace which was given me by the working of his power. To me, though I am the very least of the saints, his grace was given, to preach to the Gentiles the unsearchable riches of Christ and to make all men see what is the plan of the mystery hidden for ages in God who created all things; that through the church the manifold wisdom of God might be made known to the principalities and powers in heavenly places. This was according to the eternal purpose which he has realised in Christ Jesus our Lord, in whom we have boldness and confidence of access through our faith in him. So I ask you not to lose heart over what I am suffering for you, which is your glory.

— **EPHESIANS** 3:1-13

22

FOR THE CHURCH

The Bible says,

*And he has put all things under his feet and has made him the head
over all things for the church, which is his body, the fullness of him
who fills all in all* (Ephesians 1:22,23).

Christ has been made the head of all things for the church. There are
a number of Christians who take the church very lightly. They have a
very independent spirit. It is a mortal state. God has not done all that
he has done for just one individual. He has done it for the church.
The eyes of God are turned towards His coming kingdom. The
coming reign has to do, not with some man, however great, but with
the church.

The local church is the miniature of the universal church. You can
only treat the local church lightly to your own undoing. And, no one
who ignores the local church can take the universal church seriously.
The eyes of God turn toward His glory, power and fullness in relation
to the church. Outside of the church, it can only be death. Even if for
some time one may seem to make progress outside of the church, it
will last only for a while.

The purposes of God are tied to the church. The exaltation of Christ
has the church in view. It has nothing else in view. God has the

church in mind. In a sense, He has only the church in mind. He does not have individual believers in mind, even if they are very consecrated and holy.

Unless I find my place in the church, in the local context, I have missed it all; I am out of His purpose. Unless I see myself, my character, and my work in the context of that which God has set Christ as the head, I have missed it. It is from this perspective that the Lord Jesus could say,

> *I will build my church, and the gates of hell will not triumph over her*
> (Matthew 16:18).

The gates of hell will not triumph over the church. But they will triumph over any individual, who stands on his own. They will triumph over such a person and hold him in captivity. Could this explain some of your problems? It is the church against which the gates of hell cannot prevail. They will prevail over you if you stand outside of the church. Have you stood outside of the church, independent, and therefore not benefited from the invincibility of the church, in its conflict with the gates of hell?

The letter to the Ephesians which we are presently studying, was not written to independent individuals. It was written to the church. If you find that you are still individualistic, cry out to God, that you might see. All of God's power is available to us in the context of the church. In the church, God has given us diverse enabling for the full benefit of all.

Total power was manifested in Christ, the Head of the church. After that, God has purposed that His total power will be manifested not in the arm, foot or eye, but in the whole body, the body of Christ, which is the church. An arm that cuts itself off is ruined. A branch that cuts itself off becomes wood.

If you do not yet see, cry out to God that you may see. If you see only in part, cry out to God for greater opening of your eyes. If you think you already see to a great measure, there is yet more to see. Personally, my cry is, "God, open my eyes that I may see." Glory be to His holy name.

23

BY GRACE

*S*o that we should not boast of our place in Christ, the Bible says,

> *For by grace you have been saved through faith; and this is not your own doing, it is the gift of God - not because of works, lest any man should boast* (Ephesians 2:8-9).

Although we have been exalted in Christ, the glory for it does not go to us. It goes to God who has shown us His grace. Grace works through the mechanism of faith.

When it comes to grace, all the believer contributes is his sin. If He has no sin to contribute, then he cannot be saved. The sinner contributes his sin and God does all the rest. Then the sinner responds by faith. Even that faith is not something coming from man. You cannot congratulate yourself on having had faith. Faith is a gift of God, so that from start to finish, salvation is a work of God.

If you worked for your salvation, then you have a reason to boast. But you did not work for it. God did it all. You have nothing to glory about. You are saved, have faith and sit on the throne with Christ, but have nothing to boast of. One person did it all, the Lord. May we never lose sight of this.

It is not because we sought God, read our Bibles, that we are saved.

Many have done the same and more, but have not yet come to the salvation of the Lord Jesus. Some have read the Bible and instead confused themselves. Salvation is not a reward for reading the Bible, seeking the Lord and the like. Let us be careful else we present salvation to people as something for which they need to work for. Let us lay no conditions and barriers before men.

In some circles, they say if you are a polygamist, you must send away your wives so that you may be saved. They make salvation something for the monogamist. Often we do people the injustice of asking that they go back and put their lives right before coming to Christ. How can someone in chains put his life in order? He must first meet the Liberator, who will help him to put his life right. Sometimes we make a confession of sin a pre-requisite for salvation. There is no such thing in the scriptures. Repentance is not a recitation of all the sins you ever committed. How many can one really remember?

Repentance is a change of mind with regards to the Lord Jesus. Before, you thought He was a no-body. But now, He is everything. Before, sin was pleasurable. Now, it is horrible. Before, God looked like a tyrant wanting to hurt you. Now, He is the Father of love. There has been a change of mind.

In our testimonies of salvation, we make as though we were the heroes. In the story of the prodigal son, the son was not the hero. God the Father was the hero.

24

CREATED IN CHRIST JESUS FOR GOOD WORKS

*T*he apostle continues to say,

For we are his workmanship, created in Christ Jesus for good works,
which God prepared beforehand, that we should walk in them
(Ephesians 2:10).

The path of every believer has already been marked out by God. God has already planned the good works that we are to accomplish before His coming. Your path has been worked out already. That is His perfect will for you.

From this perspective, laziness is a terrible thing. Since God has planned what I must do every day, if I am lazy, I frustrate His purpose for that day. If I am lazy for one day, the good works for that one day will not be done. I have thereby frustrated God's purpose for one day.

Going out of God's will is the greatest tragedy that can befall anyone. Some believers have a spirit of tourism. They just enjoy visiting without purpose. By so doing they escape from the good works planned by God for them. Tourism is not a good work planned by God for any one.

Some just lie in bed day-dreaming. God certainly did not pre-plan such for anybody. Those who procrastinate are thwarting God's purpose. How dare we push forward what God wants done now? It amounts to opposing Him. What will happen with what God wanted to be done at the hour to which you have pushed the present issue?

It is as if there is a master computer in heaven and our lives have been planned second by second. Wasting time becomes criminal. The worst is using the time to do the wrong things. By such acts, we sow confusion into a System that has been very well ordered.

Look at the time you spend in anger. How will you account for it? What about the time you spend sulking or not talking to some person, out of anger? There is also the time spent carrying the cares of the world, which God never planned we should carry. How shall it be accounted for?

John Wesley said, "I have tried to give account for every five minutes of my life." He knew that time was sacred. The tragedy is to reach there with an unaccomplished mission because the time was wasted. What does God think about your use of time? What is His evaluation? For how many hours of the day can you give an account to God as used for His glory? Are you accomplishing anything? Are you using eight hours properly, but wasting sixteen? Could it be that you are lazy? Are you a big sleeper, sleeping while the war rages on? Time is the one thing you cannot recover. It is, consequently, the one thing you cannot afford to waste.

All who have not planned their time are wasting it. Some people are just at ease. They bother about nothing. There is a brother I met in one of the countries. He could get to your house at seven, have supper, chat and play his guitar till late. Reaching home, his wife would have to stand up and warm his second supper. Then he could sleep till nine a.m. the next day. For all the time I knew him, I never saw him hurry about anything. He was living without time.

I suggest that at the end of the day, you plan what should be done the next day, putting in the priority things first. Every day, week, month and year should be planned ahead of time. If the Lord tarries, do you know how you are going to use next year, years, the holidays and all the time ahead? Do you have a clear-cut plan? If you are just living from hand to mouth, you are a good fool. Even in the secular world, those who make progress are those who look ahead and plan.

We have to seek the Lord, find these good works, get His method for accomplishing them and discipline ourselves to ensure that they are accomplished. It will be totally unacceptable to get to heaven with an unaccomplished mission.

If you are wasting minutes and hours now, you will not accomplish your mission. If you sleep away the hours, you will not accomplish your mission. If you travel for every bit of nonsense, you will not accomplish your mission.

THE MYSTERY MADE KNOWN

*T*he Jews thought only in relation to themselves. In the Old Testament, God was dealing in relation to a nation. He chose that nation. The problem is that they limited God's purpose to what they saw. They did not perceive that the purpose of God was far wider than what they thought. God's purpose had gone beyond the limits of the old Israel. With the coming of the Lord Jesus, a major change was introduced. The gospel now had to be preached, beginning from Jerusalem, to Judea, all Samaria and to the ends of the earth.

You can then understand Peter's reluctance in the trance when he was told to kill and eat what was considered by the Jews to be unclean. In the same light, when the Holy Spirit came upon the Gentiles in Cornelius' house, Peter has to go back and explain things to the Jewish brethren. The coming of the Holy Spirit upon the Gentiles had taken everybody by surprise. Left on his own, Peter would not have gone to the Gentiles. But God had taken over to make the Jew and the Gentile one new man.

PAUL, A MINISTER OF THE GOSPEL

*T*hen Paul says,

Of this gospel I was made a minister according to the gift of his grace which was given me by the working of his power (Ephesians 3:7).

The word minister here is better read slave. The ministers of God are His slaves. If you want to be among the great men of God, be a servant. If you want to be among the greatest, be a slave. This is totally contrary to human logic.

Paul was called to serve by a gift of God's grace. He did not condescend to serve. He considered it a great privilege, a gift. To be allowed to serve Christ; to be God's slave is a great gift. The tragedy today is that people consider serving the Lord low-quality work. Many of those who want to serve the Lord are told to think about their future. They are warned not to waste their lives. They are told not to go too far.

The greater problem is that a number of believing parents stand on the way of their children who want to go the whole way with the Lord. They daily bring the world before them and compare them with their unbelieving friends. They simply say, "Do not take God too seriously." Where are the parents who will tell their children,

"Think first of the future of God, of the interests of God?" How can it be explained, that it is in the church, that people who want to give their utmost to God find barriers? How come that it is in the church that the "virtues" of the world are pointed to? This spells out the estimation that many Christians have of the King of glory.

Paul knew he did not deserve being gifted as a minister of the gospel of Christ. Who can deserve it? Is it not the highest honour to go to the Gentiles for Him. God had taken over to make the Jew and the Gentile one new man. Is it not the highest honour to serve Him, to live for Him, to take villages, tribes, kingdoms and nations for Him? If a man said, "I conquered a tribe" in a worldly war, they attribute greatness to him. But when a child wants to conquer a tribe for God, Christian parents think it is a waste. This must be repented of.

27

THE WORKING OF HIS POWER

*J*n calling Paul to the ministry, God honoured him.

To me, though I am the very least of all the saints, this grace was given, to preach to the Gentiles the unsearchable riches of Christ (Ephesians 3:8).

It was a miracle, the working of God's great might, to call a man to become a slave of God. People are looking for miracles, but block the greater miracle, which consists in a man becoming a slave of God. The slaves of God have decided that God would have His whole way in their lives.

To whom was the great miracle of God demonstrated? Paul says,

To me, though I am the very least of the saints...

We may categorise the saints thus:

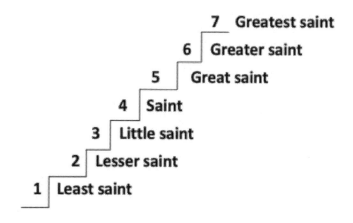

7 Greatest saint
6 Greater saint
5 Great saint
4 Saint
3 Little saint
2 Lesser saint
1 Least saint

Paul placed himself at the level of the least of all the saints. The privilege was not given to the greatest saint. Grace was given to the least of the saints to preach the unsearchable riches of Christ to the Gentiles and to make all men see the plan of the mystery of God, hidden for ages.

The revelation of God in all its totality can come to one who is the least of the saints. No one in the church should say, "I am not a great saint, far from being the greatest of the saints." If you are the least of the saints, you qualify for all the unsearchable riches of Christ. You qualify for all the manifold wisdom of God. No one needs to exclude himself.

The manifold grace of God came right to Paul who was the very least of the saints. The totality of God's grace and power worked in him to proclaim the plan of the mystery hidden for ages in God. What is your estimation of yourself? Are you the least of the saints? Then you are in good company - the company of Paul. You qualify to become a foremost apostle. Let not what you are place limitations on you. Do not regard your low estate. The least of the saints rose to enormous spiritual heights. You too can rise to spiritual heights. You can go as far as Paul went.

Stop complaining. Stop giving excuses. Stop wishing you were this or that, or that you had this gift or the other. You do not need another person's opportunities. The very least of the saints shook the world for God. You too can. He paid a price - responding to the Lord Jesus in an unusual way. He held nothing back. He smashed his career, reputation, hopes in the world, wealth, the approval of men, his right to marriage, the privilege of being understood and pursued God's call on his life. That is simply what you need to do.

The least of the saints does not become the foremost of the apostles by being at ease, doing nothing, loving the world, being divided at heart and the like. If he did not know radical and total consecration, he would go nowhere.

The problem is that many people want great things from God at no price. Where are the marks of the things you have renounced? If you do not know twenty, thirty, forty verses by heart, after three years in the Lord, because of laziness, you have disqualified yourself. You cannot make spiritual progress, unless you do something about it. How can you go for a year, leading no person to the Lord? You are barren! Worse, if this condition does not make you cry out to God for mercy, nothing will change. How can one who is at ease want to be a great man for God? The Bible says,

Woe to those who are at ease in Zion (Amos 6:1).

For there to be spiritual greatness, there needs to be a radical abandonment and sacrifice to God. Furthermore, there is need for a radical abandonment to the will of God. When a person realises that he is not growing spiritually, he must do everything, humanly speaking to improve, in the shortest possible time. Spiritual progress is not for the lazy person who does nothing about his or her poor condition.

God will not change you. You have got to change yourself. There are many things that God will not do for us. He will not pray for us, memorise the Bible for us, witness for us and so on. If we do not do them, they will remain undone. If you do not do things that make you grow, you will not grow. Some lazy believers hope to be taken along in the rapture. Never! All lazy believers will be left behind.

What are you accomplishing with your life? How long have you been in church? How much progress have you made in spiritual knowledge, in biblical knowledge, in memorising the scriptures, in personal evangelism, in holiness, at school, at your place of work? Have you been marking time in God's name?

I call you to repentance from laziness and purposelessness today. Put .an end to purposeless visiting, talking, travelling, cooking and the like. Do not be a busybody. If not, your lot will be among those whose mission was not accomplished, who did not finish their course, who did not do all that God has planned for them.

At your present rate of working, will everything be done? When God planned what you were to do, He did not make allowance for time to be wasted. In His plan, He intended that from the time of your conversion, you would set to work until you accomplish your assigned task. The time before conversion is covered under the blood. But from the time of conversion, God expects us to work with all our might, with everything in us to finish our course.

The apostle Paul says,

> But I do not account my life of any value nor as precious to myself, if only I may accomplish my course and the ministry which I received from the Lord Jesus, to testify to the gospel of the grace of God (Acts 20:24).

He put everything into it. He did not beat about the air. He said,

> Brethren, I do not consider that I have made it my own; but one thing I do, forgetting what lies behind and straining forward to what lies ahead (Philippians 3:13).

He was afraid, lest he be disqualified. And you?

Sometimes a student does work and receives from his teacher the remark, "Unsatisfactory." What is the Lord's assessment of your work? Is it satisfactory or unsatisfactory? Can we afford to get there and be told, "Unsatisfactory"? There will be no time to make up for it. Do something about it now!

CHAPTER FIVE

Therefore remember that at one time you Gentiles in the flesh, called the uncircumcision by what is called the circumcision, which is made in the flesh by hands - remember that you were at that time separated from Christ, alienated from the commonwealth of Israel, and strangers to the covenants of promise, having no hope and without God in the world. But now in Christ Jesus you who were once far off have been brought near in the blood of Christ. For he is our peace, who has made us both one, and has broken down the dividing wall of hostility, by abolishing in the flesh the law of commandments and ordinances, that he might create in himself one new man in place of the two, so making peace, and might reconcile us both to God in one body through his cross, thereby bringing the hostility to an end. And he came and preached peace to you who were far off and peace to you who were near; for through him we both have access in one spirit to the Father. So then you are no longer strangers and sojourners, but you are fellow citizens with the saints and members of the household of God, built upon the foundation of the apostles and prophets, Christ

Jesus himself being the cornerstone, in whom the whole structure is joined together and grows into a holy temple in the Lord; in whom you also are built into it for a dwelling place of God in the Spirit.

— EPHESIANS 2:11-22

THE BLOOD OF CHRIST

What were we before we came to Christ? We were:

1. Separated from Christ,
2. Alienated from the commonwealth of Israel,
3. Strangers to the covenants of promise,
4. Having no hope and
5. Without God in the world.

If things remained as described above, it would be terrible. Thank God, there is a tremendous "but" - "But now in Christ Jesus you who were once far off have been brought near in the blood of Christ." We have been brought near in the blood. Through the blood of the Lord Jesus Christ we have

1. Been united with Christ,
2. Been admitted into the commonwealth of Israel,
3. Become partakers in the covenants of promise,
4. We have a hope and
5. God in the world. Glory be to His Holy Name!

HE IS OUR PEACE

*O*ur peace is not a thing. Our peace is a Person, the Lord Jesus Christ. Some people take tranquilisers to have peace. Some drink alcohol to drown their problems. Some run away from their problems. They may refuse to greet the person with whom they have had a problem or move houses or offices to avoid one person or persons. That is not the pathway to peace.

Is there some restlessness in your heart? Do not look left or right. Turn to the Lord Jesus Christ. He is in you. He is your peace. Jesus is your peace in a restless world - a world in which everything is falling apart. Jesus is not only your peace. He left His peace with us as, our legacy. He said,

> *Peace be with you* (John 20:26);

> *Peace I leave with you; my peace I give to you; not as the world gives do I give to you. Let not your hearts be troubled, neither let them be afraid* (John 14:27).

The world may be in turmoil, experience inflation, calamities and other ills, but those who know their God are in peace. He is their peace. Say to Him, "Lord Jesus, you are my peace in a restless and unstable world, filled with changing circumstances. Thank you Lord".

My prayer is that we would know Jesus in a more intimate way, so that we might equally know His peace more intimately.

ONE NEW MAN

*T*here are two men in the Bible. The first of them is Adam. All who descend from him bear his marks. When Adam plunged the whole race into sin, everyone become a sinner. There is another man, the Lord Jesus, the Victor. He became the second Adam, and also the last Adam and the starting point of a new race.

In the present passage, the apostle Paul talks of one new man. God wants to see the church as one new man. The Bible says,

> *That he might create in himself one new man in place of the two, so making peace, and might reconcile us both to God in one body through his cross, thereby bringing the hostility to an end* (Ephesians 2:14-15).

Before, there was the Jew and then the Gentile. Both were hostile against each other and had broken the ordinances of God. Therefore, there was hostility between the two men, and between the two men and God. We may illustrate this hostility as below:

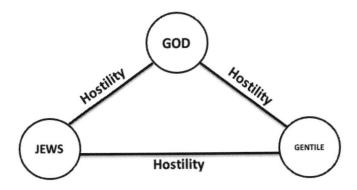

Through the cross, Jesus united the Jew to the Gentile and the Gentile to the Jew, making one new man out of the two in Himself. He reconciled both the Jew and the Gentile to God in one body, the church, bringing the hostility to an end. What happened on the cross was a very far-reaching event.

Is there enmity between you and some child of God? If there is, you are offending the cross. Do you still harbour ill-feelings against anyone? The cross has brought that hostility to an end. The barriers have been torn down. Put right every relationship that is not flowing. The Lord was lifted up on the cross to bring peace, real peace. If you have a chilly relationship with somebody, add heat to it.

If the cross broke the barrier between the Jew and the Gentile, how can fellow saints tolerate barriers among themselves? The Bible demands that we do not let the sun set while we are still angry. But some have misunderstandings and go to bed with them. What if the trumpet should sound at night? Jesus came and preached peace. May we enter into it.

31

WE ARE THE TEMPLE OF THE LORD

*W*e are the household of God. We are the temple of the Lord, a dwelling place of God in the spirit. God dwells in us by the spirit. Do you then see the implications of a believer's sin? It is as though he were taking God into sin. Where do you keep God when you want to sin? It is a frightful thing when a believer sins. He wants to take God and plunge Him into sin. The purposelessness and laziness of a believer amount to making God the same kind of person as he. The one who procrastinates reduces God to someone who thinks about the future but will not act now.

The fact that we are the dwelling place of God in the spirit places very far-reaching demands on our lives. We can no longer do anything which God would not do, or does not want done. We can no longer say, think, desire or approve what God would not or does not want.

Do you know that you carry God within you? If I had ten billion dollars on me, it would be something to reckon with. I would be utterly careful with myself. I would be fully alert. But we are not carrying dollars. Dollars are nothing. We carry God in us. He has come to dwell in us.

A lot of God's children tolerate sin in their thoughts. In their minds they tolerate that which is impure and wicked. I wonder whether they know whom they carry inside them. If a man's thoughts are not sanctified, the person is not sanctified as well. If a believer committed adultery in act, it would seem terrible. But when it is in the mind, the tendency is to take it lightly. No! It is as serious! Adultery in the mind is an attempt to suffocate the indwelling God, with so horrible a sin.

CHAPTER SIX

That through the church the manifold wisdom of God might now be made known to the principalities and powers in heavenly places. This was according to the eternal purpose which he has realised in Christ Jesus our Lord in whom we have boldness and confidence of access through our faith in him

— *EPHESIANS 3:10-13*

For this reason I bow my knees before the Father, from whom every family in heaven and on earth is named, that according to the riches of his glory he may grant you to be strengthened with might through his Spirit in the inner man, and that Christ may dwell in your hearts through faith; that you, being rooted and grounded in love, may have power to comprehend with all the saints what is the breath and length and height and depth, and to know the love of Christ which surpasses knowledge, that you may be filled with all the fullness of God. Now to him who by the power at work within us is able to do far more abundantly than all that we ask or think, to him be glory in the church and in Christ Jesus to all generations, forever and ever. Amen.

— EPHESIANS 3:14-21

32

THE MANIFOLD WISDOM OF GOD -1

When I started preparing these messages, my thoughts went to the realm of miracles. I thought that when the lame walk and the like, the manifold wisdom of God is being displayed to principalities and powers. But these last few days, the Lord has been showing me that His heart is more concerned with something else. Actually, there is a battle, an inward battle - the world's desire to arrest the believer and reign over him or her, the desire of sin to reign in the life of the believer.

I also came to realise that the purpose of God is that the believer should give a technical knockout to the world, the flesh and the devil, to the praise of God. The manifold wisdom of God is made known to principalities and powers by a walk with God that puts the devil to flight.

We are surrounded by a multitude of angels watching, good and bad. When a believer entertains wicked thoughts, the very purpose of God is frustrated because principalities and powers are watching and they know the battles involved. When there is purity, the manifold wisdom of God is manifested. You recall that the eternal purpose of God is that we might be holy and blameless before Him.

This means that if principalities and powers come with some temptation and the believer falls prey in his mind to this temptation, he worships the devil. There is therefore no manifestation of the manifold wisdom of God in that believer. The battle is, consequently, not an outward battle. It is an inner one. Where there is lust, the battle is lost. In such a case, the principalities and powers cannot see the manifold wisdom of God.

When you look at the temptation of the Lord Jesus by the devil, it is obvious that it took place in His mind. The devil did not physically take Him to the temple in Jerusalem, because these temptations took place when the Lord was in the wilderness. The greatest battles were in His inner being. As with the Lord, the believer's fiercest battles are in the inward being. It is in the inward being that principalities and powers are to have their technical knockout. Before a man fails outwardly, he has already failed inwardly. The one who wins inwardly, will win outwardly.

It may be the battle to compromise, to lie a bit, to surrender. It may be the battle with the world's desires and claims, or its passing glory. It could be the battle with the will of God, especially when that will contradicts the believer's own desires.

What is the testimony of principalities and powers as far as you are concerned? Is it, "We cannot seduce this one?" Can they say, "We have offered this and that, but he is beyond our seduction?" Or, have you been bought? Have you yielded? Have you surrendered to sin, to the world, to the desires of the flesh, to covetousness and the passing glory of the world? If that is the case, then the manifold wisdom of God cannot be shown to the principalities and powers through you.

What do the principalities and powers say about you?

- What do they say about what is happening in your mind?
- What do they say about your commitment?
- What do they say about your desires?
- What do they say about your motives?
- What do they say about your sense of direction?

These questions are of the utmost importance. Notice that what matters in the conflict with principalities and powers is not what the brethren think about you. They may mistakenly think that you are a wonder. That does not deceive the principalities and powers. You know, and they also know where the problem lies.

In Obala, Cameroon, the brethren were carrying out a deliverance from demons. One sister moved up and commanded the demons to come out. The demons disobeyed and said to her, "You are just like us." This is the testimony of demons. They look through us and decide whether they should fear us or not. How can they fear a believer with a half-hearted commitment to the Lord? Would they fear a believer who wants heaven but also wants the world? They cannot. They would point to the worldliness in his heart because he is like them.

When demons find a totally obedient person, they are impotent because that is where they failed. We are not told that the spirits that failed disobeyed in everything. They disobeyed in as much as the Lordship of Jesus was concerned. Therefore, where there is no unconditional yielding to the Lordship of Jesus, there is no power over principalities and powers. When the Lordship of Jesus is lacking in a believer's life, his words against demons are powerless. Such a believer can bind demons a million times and nothing happens.

The only means to have power over demons is to render unconditional obedience to the Lord Jesus. Demons will obey us in proportion to our degree of obedience to the Lord Jesus. When our obedience is complete, they will equally obey us instantaneously. In this manner, we can display the manifold wisdom of God to the principalities and powers.

Are there some people, who will cry out to God so that we show forth the manifold wisdom of God to principalities and powers? Will God have co-workers who will put demons in their rightful place? If He does not find them, His victory will remain as though He never won. Yet He did win and has lifted us up with Christ, so that His victory may be manifested through us. The slightest disobedience on your, our and my part is considered high treason.

Disobedience is the determination to frustrate all of God's purposes. I need not disobey in many things in order to be disqualified. One act of disobedience is enough for the principalities and powers to begin to ignore me, worst of all, to mock Christ. The church must totally come back to living under the Lordship of Jesus, and then principalities and powers will be no equal to her might.

THE MANIFOLD WISDOM OF GOD - 2

I have been looking at the loss of power in church history, as compared to the power manifested in the early church. One thing is striking – in the early church, sin was judged very severely. When the Holy Spirit moved unchallenged, Annanias and Sapphira lied, and God judged them with death. The lives of the brethren in the early church was such that a lie was a terrible thing. Only in such a church can the Holy Spirit find His place. If we are going to see the Holy Spirit move again in might, something must happen in our lives with regards to our attitude to sin and the Lordship of Jesus.

Annanias did not only lie. He was worldly. His lie was a betrayal of his worldliness. Where there is worldliness, there is also an Annanias and, or a Sapphira. Where there is worldliness, the church is blocked. My prayer to God is that something radical would happen in each life in the church. May we rend our hearts before God and seek Him with all of our hearts. May we not take any rest until we have found Him with all of our hearts. May we seek him in spirit and in truth and find no rest until we have found Him in all of His fullness.

Could it be that we have been deceived to think that it is only unbelievers who should seek God? The Psalmist's heart panted, burned and longed for God, the living God. Paul said,

That I may know him and the power of his resurrection, and may
share his sufferings, becoming like him in his death, that if possible,
I may attain the resurrection from the dead (Philippians
3:10-11).

Why has such seeking for God disappeared from many hearts and
lives in the church? Where are those who will wait on Him and
promise not to leave until He blesses them? Where are those who
will spend one hour and come again for a second, third, fourth and
keep coming until anew they find their Beloved? Do we still miss our
Beloved? Do we still miss His presence? Could it be that we have
begun to practise a magic formula with the Lord wherein we think
we can just recite a few words and expect everything to come back to
normal? Has such a formula stripped us of the desire to seek and
yearn after Him?

Are there some who will press on in search of the Beloved and not
accept a false comfort? Are there some who will not accept words of
encouragement from man, rather would labour to hear the Beloved
Himself speak words of encouragement to them? Are there modern
Jacobs, who will spend the whole night wrestling with angels and
until they reach breakthrough at day break?

Where are the lovers of God? Where are those who are not just satisfied with a judicial position before God? Have we become like a
woman who is satisfied with her wedding ring or marriage certificate
without knowing the warmth of her husband? What about the presence of the Lord Jesus felt and experienced? What about His spirit
flowing through our spirits or His word to us saying, "Son you are
mine?" Has such a word ceased in your life, so that you have accepted
the routine? Or, have you never known it?

Have you fallen into the trap of using scripture to justify your spiritual dryness? Have you justified your disobedience and the lack of the
knowledge of Him? Are you satisfied with some spiritual gift(s)
without the Giver? Have you become like a woman satisfied with a
doll, whereas she needs a child of her own? Where are the barren
women who will each say, "Give me children or I die?"

Where are those who will accept nothing else until there is break-through in their relationship with Jesus? They must come up to the scene and must do that, urgently. I do not know how much time we still have to go before the Lord of glory is here. But can it still be long? Is there any certainty that we are not at the end? Is there?

Should we not put aside everything else and seek God? Should we not be restless until we find our rest in Him? Should we not refuse all comfort from anybody until He comforts us? Should we not press on for our lost inheritance? Shall we be satisfied because we compare ourselves with others? May a new day dawn in the church when the lovers of the Lord would seek and not rest until they have found Him. As they find Him, may they be led to seek Him in more intense ways.

May everything that stands in the way be torn down and every barrier removed. May we stop knowing about Him and rather get down to knowing Him. May we give Him no rest until He tears off the veil that separates us from Him and shows us His glory. May we knock and knock until we wear Him out until we get to the point where He cannot but do something for us. May we accept no cheap solution, because He offers no cheap solutions. May we refuse to be deceived.

O, that we would rend our hearts and wear sackcloth, yearning, refusing to be comforted until He comforts us! May He open our eyes to see our present poverty. May He begin with you today. May He begin with the church today. May this continue in the church until the Bride is made ready, without spot, blemish and wrinkle. May it continue until the Lamb's Bride is burning, yearning, spending every minute watching and waiting for His return. When this happens, He will come quickly, and the yearning hearts will be satisfied. It is only this kind of Bride that can show forth the manifold wisdom of God to the principalities and powers.

34

GOD HAS BANKED ON THE CHURCH

*W*e have seen that it is God's purpose that through the church, the manifold wisdom of God might be made known to the principalities and powers. We saw that it was first of all an inner work, so that the devil might find in us a people he cannot trap. We have seen that we ought to be people totally separated and consecrated to the Lord, totally liberated from sin and all bondages. The apostle saw this and said it was a mystery hidden in times past, but that now God has chosen to reveal it. This mystery is according to God's purpose in Christ Jesus.

Knowing the above, the apostle says,

> *For this reason I bow my knees before the Father, from whom every family in heaven and on earth is named* (Ephesians 3:14-15).

He knew the tremendous place of the church in the heart of God. It is as if in Christ, God has finished the battle with the enemy and now tells the church to show the principalities and powers what He has done. It is like a father who tells his son, "Go and show this man my power, my wealth, my authority."

God is not afraid that the church may fail. I am amazed at the confidence that He has in the church. God is not worried about the church. He is confident that the church will win. The church will surely show the manifold wisdom of God to the principalities and powers. God believes the church and takes her to heart. Before God, it is impossible that the church should fail.

Why does God not worry about the Christian church? It is because He does not worry about what Christ did at Calvary and what was accomplished in the resurrection and in the enthronement of Christ. He is totally relaxed because the church has been raised with Christ in glory. There is no cause for worry. You too should not worry about the church. Let me take this further – God does not worry about you, as a member of the body of Christ. He knows you will make it to the end, and be presented without spot, blemish or wrinkle with the rest of the church. God is perfectly at peace about you. You, too, should be totally at peace about yourself.

The call to seek the Lord is not a call to worry. Be at rest and at peace about yourself, as God is. Let me ask you this question: Why isn't God worried about you and me? Because He has full confidence in our union and identification with Christ. The Bible says,

> *For if we have been united with him in a death like his, we shall certainly be united with him in a resurrection like his* (Romans 6:5)

> *But if we have died with Christ, we believe that we shall also live with him* (Romans 6:8).

We shall be united with Him in His kingdom and reign. We shall make it to the end. I pray that you may have this assurance and that you might enter into the rest of God. Only those who seek God from a position of rest may find Him.

WE ARE BORN OF GOD

*T*hey call me Fomum after my father. That is that for sonship to my earthly father. We also find a name such as Simon Barjonah, meaning Simon the son of Jonah. Coming to our new birth, every believer's name is followed, in essence, by BarGod. The believer is named after God because he is born of God,

> *Whosoever believeth that Jesus is the Christ is born of God ...* (1 John 5:1, KJV).

This carries with it a lot of weight and privileges. If you were the son of a President, you will certainly enjoy some privileges. How much more when you are the son of God Most High!

We are linked to the Father by birth. We are His, even in our weakest of moments. When a child fails, does he lose childhood to the parents? Are you God's child only when you do the right things? Such will be a very poor relationship. We carry the genes of God in us, which He imparted to us through Christ. All of us who have come to Christ are His children and are named after Him. May we never doubt it. One of the tools in the hands of the devil is doubt. He uses it against the children of God to make them doubt their place in their relationship with God. May we not allow him to deceive us anymore.

STRENGTHENED IN THE INNER MAN

*P*aul prayed that according to the riches of God's glory, He may grant the brethren to be strengthened with might through God's Spirit in the inner man. The Holy Spirit comes in to strengthen. He comes to give power over sin, self, the love of the world and the love of the things that are in the world. The power in the inner man is first of all the power to make us conform to Christ in our being. It is power unto Christ-likeness in character. One of the elements in the character of Christ is selflessness. In His prayer, He never asked anything for Himself, except once, when He asked that the cup be taken away from Him. Even then, He bowed to the Father's will immediately afterwards.

How is your own prayer life? How much of it turns around yourself? The degree of your selfishness in prayer is an indication of the level of your maturity. As people grow and mature in the Lord, they ask less and less for themselves, but more and more for the glory of the Lord. Look at your prayer list, and it will tell you how big you are. You may find that after many years in the Lord, you are only a baby. The baby's list of requests consists in, "Give me this; give me that; give me the other; give me those; give me more."

We are to be strengthened in the inner man so that self might give way to Christ. The aim is,

Not I, but Christ? (Galatians 2:20, KJV).

We are also to be strengthened in the inner man so that we may know how to yield, beholding Him on Calvary, who for us bowed His head and died.

If there are problems between you and your wife, husband, child, friend, it is surely a problem of the self. The problems are a reflection of unsurrendered lives. The greater person yields. He does not insist on his rights. He surrenders and dies to self[1]. Have you learnt to surrender? What happens when you discover that someone is wanting to cheat you? If you insist too much on your rights, you will not know peace. Yield, surrender your rights and you will make progress with the Lord.

Is someone using you? Stop complaining about it or about the person. Go a second mile. Yield and you will grow. When did you last disagree with someone? You will find that if you had surrendered, not insisting on your own way, things might have been different. Could it be that you are the problem? Then yield if you are.

Are you waiting for some junior person to come and apologise or repent to you? The one who takes the first step towards reconciliation is the greater person. How great are you? The senior person who will not take the first step to reconciliation is the bigger fool. He is the bigger problem. The husband who always waits for his wife to take the first step to reconciliation is losing his authority. His wife will ultimately rule the home.

When we look at the Lord Jesus, He took the first and all the other steps down to have us reconciled to the Father. He was the greater person and took the first step. Even about little things like greeting, some people only wait for the other party to first greet them. They are really small.

Some people do not know how to say, "I am sorry." These are perhaps the smallest of persons. If you meet such a person, you have met one who is very near being a fool. Some may call it pride, - well, pride and foolishness grow on the same tree.

In the work of the Holy Spirit to strengthen the believer in the inner man, the believer is given power over sin. The power of sin is broken deep inside of the person. He knows consistent and continuous victory over sin. Through the working of the Holy Spirit, the very idea of sin is fought from inside and victory is won, so that the believer does not go battling with acts of sin. He has triumphed in the inner man.

Look around and you will realise that many of God's children are very inclined towards the love of the world. The world seems to have a real pull on them. It should not be so. The believer should be strengthened in the inner man. Normally, the Holy Spirit builds a barrier, so that the world finds it difficult to penetrate the believer. It should be that the devil finds a hard time using anything in the world to tempt the believer.

The purpose of God is to produce a people in the church whom Satan cannot easily have access to. God wants the church to be made of people before whom the devil is sure to fail in his attempts to overcome them. The church should normally go from strength to strength as the strengthening work of the Holy Spirit continues. The work of the Holy Spirit is continuous, and so must the saints move from strength to strength in the inner man.

The purpose of God is that we should continue, in an increasing manner, to be strengthened in our inner man, by the Holy Spirit. We must, in an increasing way, be delivered from self, sin and the love of the world. Although the strengthening work of God could come as a crisis, it is followed by a continuous process.

There must come a day in the life of a believer when there is a crisis dealing with God with regard to the world. But this must be followed by a continuous experience of growing victory over the world. God is ready to do this according to the riches of His glory. And, how rich His glory is!

THE RICHES OF HIS GLORY

God wants to strengthen us in the inner man according to the riches of His glory. That is what He wants to do for you. He is at work in you. He will do it for you in the measure of Christ. Tell God, "Father, I am prepared to cooperate with you, so that in full measure, as found in the Lord Jesus Christ, I might be strengthened in the inner man." Yes, strengthened in the inner man, and flowing naturally.

The power of the Lord Jesus Christ flowed. He was not agitated. His life, His word and His acts flowed. The power in His inner man flowed through the outer man and through the outermost man. In other words, the power in the inner man flowed through His spirit, soul and body. I say this because, sometimes you find some people in whom there is some power of God who gesticulate wildly and twist themselves unnaturally. This could be some display to draw attention or that God's power flowing through them meets with obstacles. The deeper the river, the quieter the flow.

FAITH IN THE DWELLING CHRIST

*P*aul also prayed that the saints might have faith; "That Christ may dwell in your hearts through faith." There is faith to receive the Lord Jesus Christ in salvation, but there is also faith for the Lord Jesus Christ to dwell in the believer and take possession of him.

Everything depends on faith. We must believe that when we prayed and asked Him to come into our hearts, He did. He is right there, deep down in our hearts. Would He stand at the door knocking, only to walk away when we open our hearts to Him? No.

Our faith must grow from conversion faith to the faith that allows the Lord Jesus Christ to fully dwell in us. As we believe it for ourselves, we must not doubt the conversion and dwelling presence of God in the hearts and lives of others who profess Christ. More and more in some circles, you hear that someone has made a decision to follow the Lord. No! The person has been converted. He has received salvation. He has become a child of God! We must not speak in doubt about what God is doing in the lives of others.

Another thing I notice is that there are some who keep asking Jesus to come into their lives and save them. They doubt that when at first they genuinely asked Him to come into their hearts, He did come. That is lack of faith. It must not be so. Still, others who are convinced of their salvation keep asking the Lord to come and take possession of them. He is not a deaf Christ. A person should consecrate his life to the Lord and surrender to Him once. Afterwards, the surrender may only need to be reaffirmed, not doubted.

Let us not seem to want a new kind of transaction with the Lord every blessed day. May God grant us faith, without which Christ will not dwell in us. It is one thing for Christ to come in, but another for Him to dwell, to take possession and to be at home in our hearts. He will not take more possession when we multiply our activities. He takes possession as we believe Him, as we surrender our lives to Him. May we believe that He takes our surrender to Him seriously and thank Him for accepting us.

We must be so convinced that our faith becomes a weapon against the enemy. We must hold so firm to our faith in the indwelling Christ that the enemy has no room to inject any doubts into us. Even when we fail, He never fails. All we need to do is to reaffirm our loyalty to Him. We are to reaffirm and confess that we are His. We are never to doubt that we are His. Let us confess to Him that we are His. Let us confess that He fully dwells in us. In this way, we give Him room to dwell in us in an ever-increasing way.

39

Rooted has to do with developing depth. Grounded has to do with being well settled, not easily shaken. The believer needs to comprehend the breadth, length, depth and height of the love of God. God's love for us is wider than breadth, longer than length, deeper than depth and higher than height.

How many of God's children do not know that God loves them? How many are not assured of His love for them? How many look at Him as though He were some stern man with a stick raised over them, to hit them with should the least mistake be made? How many do not perceive His love? How many fail to enjoy His love because they doubt it? How many measure God's love from the perspective of their own limited capacity to love? May God give us grace to comprehend His love for us.

There will never be a circumstance in which God stops to love us. God never goes away from us, rather, we may go away from Him, not the other way round. His love is unchanging. Our love may change, His love remains intact. Did you know this?

Even when we are unwilling, His love abides. His love remains strong and firm even when we are fickle. May you know that God's love for you as a person and for us as His children is without limits. Do not be fooled to think that His love for some persons is without limits, but that towards you it is limited. Why must He single you out for disfavour? His love towards you is without limits. Because of Christ, God's love for each one of us is without limits.

There is nothing you can do to get beyond the reach of God's love. In the darkest night and in the deepest failure, fall back into His loving arms. Even when you deny Him as Peter did, He looks at you with eyes that are full of love.

Have you ever been picked up from the depths of failure? Have you ever felt at some moment that the only thing you deserved was the lake of fire? As a believer, have you ever fallen to such depths that you got to think that if God forgave you He would be doing injustice? But did you not later see His love flow and overtake you? Indeed, His love is an unchanging love. He is faithful.

I have personally known that love flowing out to me in my darkest moments and in my deepest failure. I have known it when I was in total loneliness. His hand reaches out and touches us where no one could reach out and touch us. He flows to us in love at moments when were our failure made known, some people would crucify us.

We are not only to know about the love of God. We are to experience it, and be filled with the fullness of God. Those who go the furthest are those who know this love. I have never seen a man who doubted his salvation do anything outstanding for God. I have never seen a man who is not sure that God loves him, make spiritual progress. I have never seen anybody who thought that God did not love him much, grow to spiritual heights.

All who have made progress with God are people who knew, in an unshakable way, that at their worst, God loved them and that He did not change His mind about loving them. Driven by such confidence, though their paths were spotted with failure, they moved ahead to do near-impossible things for God.

Rise out of your mediocrity. Rise out of your failure, out of your backsliding, weariness, hopelessness, despair and sin. How long have you wallowed in these? How long will you continue in gloom and despondency? Put an end to the past, and fall back into the arms of the Eternal Lover, and let a new day begin. His love has conquered.

As far as the east is from the west, so far has He removed our sin from us. He has taken away the separating wall. Jump out into His love and victory for you. Come back to the Lord and rest in His love. How deep and how assuring it is! Come!

CHAPTER SEVEN

I therefore, a prisoner for the Lord, beg you to lead a life worthy of the calling to which you have been called, with all lowliness and meekness, with patience, forbearing one another in love, eager to maintain the unity of the Spirit in the bond of peace. There is one body and one Spirit, just as you were called to the one hope that belongs to your call, one Lord, one faith, one baptism, one God and Father of us all, who is above all and through all in all.

— EPHESIANS 4:1-6

40

OUR CALLING AS BELIEVERS

If we do not enjoy our inheritance in Christ for whatever reason, it remains our inheritance. Nothing can change that which we are in Christ, but the Father's good pleasure is that we should enjoy it. Even if a prince lived like a beggar, he remains a prince. But it is better if he entered into his inheritance and enjoyed his status of a prince.

I say this because many of us would deny that someone is a prince only because he is living like a beggar. He is a prince, only that he is not enjoying the privileges there attached. On the other hand, a man does not become a prince because he lives like a prince. If a beggar should be given princely clothes and even a luxurious car, will this make him a prince?

The first and most crucial thing is what God has made of us. We must focus on who we are in Christ, before looking at the outward implications. Sometimes we forget God and become rationalistic in our thinking. Is a child of God the person who never fails? No!

We may not be fully living out what we are, but it does not cancel who we are. From knowing and being committed to who we are, we will rise up to live as we ought to. If you see a believer sinning, rebuke him because he is a child of God. It is wrong to conclude that since you saw him sinning, he is not a child of God.

Being a believer or not is first of all dependent on what God has done. Unless we see things this way, we shall think that some very good unbelievers will have the first seats in heaven. The most generous, kind and temperate man I know is not a believer. It is difficult to make him angry. But he remains an enemy of the Lord who died on the cross. He does not believe in the only begotten Son of God. His good character does not bring him one bit nearer to the Lord.

The believer who is indwelt by the Lord Jesus is an eternity better than the well-behaved unbeliever. A child may fall into mud and rub himself in it, but a very clean pig can never be mistaken for a human child. Though faeces be rubbed on you and you are stinking, you remain far better than the best dressed corpse in the most sophisticated casket costing millions. This is why the apostle first deals with our position in Christ before he comes to talk about the outworking of this position.

41

A LIFE WORTHY OF OUR CALLING

*H*e says,

*I, therefore, a prisoner for the Lord, beg you to lead a life worthy of
the calling to which you have been called* (Ephesians 4:1).

You have been called. Your call comes first; that is, your place in the
Lord Jesus Christ. Only in response to the call can you live a life
worthy of the calling. If you are not called, you may imitate the life-
style of those who have been called, but that does not make you a
called person.

Sin is not worthy of the life to which we have been called. Therefore,
we throw it all away. The one question to ask about anything is
whether it is worthy of our calling. If not, it is to be thrown away.
Would you wear a beard of monkey fur? If by some chance you
discover that you have such a beard on, what do you do? You tear it
off and throw it away. Sin is like monkey-fur worn on your beard.
Turn to the Lord in prayer. Repent of all that is monkey-fur to your
human body. You can be sure that He will forgive you because the
Bible says,

*If we confess our sins, he is faithful and just, and will forgive our sins
and cleanse us from all unrighteousness* (1 John 1: 10).

This message was written to believers who happen to fall in sin. It was not to unbelievers since their whole life is simply sin. The unbeliever's very being is sin. He only has to fall before God and plead for mercy. But the believer can confess his or her sin and be sure to be forgiven.

42

LOWLINESS AND MEEKNESS

We are to live the Christian life in all lowliness and meekness, forbearing one another in love. Lowliness is a mark of great people. Fools lift themselves up. It is the small who need to lift themselves up and seek for notice. Some write their names and try to attack all the degrees and titles they ever had because their names alone mean nothing. Humility is a mark of greatness.

Meekness is the capacity to hold great talent in check. Those who are capable of nothing cannot be meek. What would they be holding in check? Humility is not for those who have nothing. Look at the Lord Jesus Christ. He was the Lord of glory. He had power to do everything. But He did not use His power for Himself. He could blast His enemies with one word. But He did not. He had tremendous powers which He held under control. That is meekness.

Do not be a mediocrity and mistake it for meekness. Meekness implies great capacities, great potentials, great power held under control. There is a story about a beloved brother from the University of Yale. He could have become anything he wanted in life. He had education, money and youthfulness. He was a millionaire at twenty-four in those days. But he chose to go to South East Asia in order to win the Moslems there to the Lord Jesus. He was meek. He held great power in check. He did not go there because he lacked a job. He was not like those who, finding nothing else in the world to do, say they want to serve God. He deliberately turned his back on what the world could offer. He refused to have what he could have of the world.

43

WITH PATIENCE, FORBEARING ONE ANOTHER

$\mathcal{T}$he apostle talks about patience in relation to meekness − because those with great abilities often find it difficult to deal with people who are dim-witted. Great abilities often go with impatience. Well, there are some very impatient unable persons. But the very able have to cultivate patience as they relate with those who are slow or do not see.

Forbearing means that there will be things in other people that do not conform to what we think or approve. The smart will need to forbear the slow and the gentle should bear with those who are rough. God's variety is amazing. Look at your assembly and see how diverse you are. We are so different that we need to bear with one another. Some people sing and clap and jump and rejoice. Others just clap gently on the spot. In actual fact, both types of persons need to bear with one another.

We have different temperaments, and the Holy Spirit takes them into consideration as He deals with us. Let us not make a mistake or make judgements on the basis of temperament. Let us bear one another, irrespective of temperamental differences.

Love makes forbearance flow from the heart in truth. If there is no love, you cannot forbear. There must be the witness of the Holy Spirit deep down in you, that love is at the base of your forbearance of the brethren. If love is lacking, you may seem to be forbearing, but nothing will come out of it. If you condemn the brethren in your heart, you are already guilty. God looks at what is in the heart.

44

EAGER TO MAINTAIN THE UNITY OF THE SPIRIT

*T*he Bible does not talk of creating unity. It talks of maintaining unity. Why? Because all true believers are united. We only maintain that which already exists. There are two main grounds on which rests the unity of the saints. The first of the reasons is that the Lord Jesus prayed that all His may be one. His prayer could not have gone unanswered because He prayed in the centre of God's will. Secondly, all true believers belong to the one body of the Lord. The body is one and holds together.

May God open our eyes to see that there is but one body of Christ. Regardless of what you think about any truly converted brothers and sisters, they are in the body, and therefore are a part of you. Whether you like some parts of the body or not, they are there. The most rational thing to do is to love every part of the body because there are no two bodies of Christ.

Whatever you call yourself in Christ – Pentecostal, Protestant, or Redeemed and so on, you are Christian and belong to the one body of the children of God. You and I are believers in the Lord Jesus Christ. We belong to the Lord Jesus Christ and to His one body.

The Lord Jesus Christ said,

And I have other sheep, that are not of this fold; I must bring them also, and they will heed my voice. So there shall be one flock, one shepherd (John 10:16).

There is one flock and one Shepherd. There are not two flocks and two Shepherds.

We belong to all who belong to the Lord Jesus Christ. All who belong to the Lord Jesus Christ belong to us. Out of short-sightedness or ignorance, some believers may reject us. Never mind, they still remain one with us in Christ! May we never reject anyone who belongs to the Lord Jesus Christ. We are under obligation to accept all whom the Lord Jesus Christ accepts and to reject all whom He rejects.

This does not mean that all believers are of the same degree of maturity, have the same proximity to the Lord of glory, have the same level of understanding and proclamation of the truth. If you have children, all will not have the same level of bodily cleanliness, but all are your children. Some will be closer to you than others. Some will obey you more whole-heartedly than others. But all are your children.

If the hardworking child told the one who is lazy, "You do not belong to Papa and Mama", how would you, the father, take it? It is true that the other child is lazy, but has the hard-working child the right to exclude the lazy one? Who gave him such powers?

All believers will not have the same reward. Those who love the Lord more, obey the truth more, go the whole way with the Lord and so on. will have greater recompense and be closer to Him in all eternity. But may we not leave out any who are His.

Some believers are a bit on the blind end. Some are almost totally blind about a number of issues. However, if they bear the mark that they are His, with the witness of the Holy Spirit that they have passed from death to life, they should be accepted into the brotherhood of all the saints. The same Holy Spirit dwells in all believers.

Some teach that there are believers who do not have the Holy Spirit. Such a doctrine must be directly from hell. Before a person becomes a believer, the Holy Spirit comes and woes him to Jesus. When the person opens up to Christ, the Holy Spirit comes in, imparts the new life and dwells in the person. When you say, "Lord Jesus, come into my life", He comes in, in the person of the Holy Spirit. The Lord Jesus Christ does not come Himself to dwell in you. The one who dwells in you is the Holy Spirit. The Lord Jesus Christ is on the throne.

To put it in other words, when Jesus Christ ascended, in some sense, His era ended. Pentecost signalled the beginning of the era of the Holy Spirit. Before Bethlehem, even though God the Father, God the Son and God the Holy Spirit lived together, it was God the Father operating. From Bethlehem, in His dealings with men, until the Ascension, God the Son was operating. From Pentecost, God the Holy Spirit has been operating.

But the Lord Jesus Christ is going to come back personally, physically, to reign. Until He comes back to reign physically, it is the Holy Spirit at work. Nevertheless, to have the Holy Spirit dwelling in you and to be baptised or filled with the Holy Spirit are different spiritual experiences.

Although the Holy Spirit dwells in all believers, not all believers are baptised into the Holy Spirit. Of all those who are baptised into the Holy Spirit, not all are filled with the Holy Spirit. The question is, "Do you belong to the Lord Jesus Christ?" If yes, the Holy Spirit dwells in you. But that is not the end. Go ahead and be baptized into the Holy Spirit and then be filled with the Holy Spirit. Remain filled with the Holy Spirit.

45

ONE HOPE, ONE LORD, ONE FAITH, ONE BAPTISM

*W*e have read that,

There is one body and one Spirit, just as you were called to the one hope that belongs to your call, one Lord, one faith, one baptism, one God and Father of us all, who is above all and through all and in all (Ephesians 4:4-6).

There is not one Lord for my brother and another for me. There is not one Lord for one group of believers and another Lord for another group. O that God may arise and pull down the barriers that the enemy has established among His children!

Some people say the one baptism is the baptism of the Holy Spirit. That is false! The Bible says,

For by one Spirit we were all baptized. Into one body - Jews or Greeks, slaves or free - and all mere made to drink of one Spirit (1 Corinthians 12:13).

In the baptism into the one body, the Holy Spirit takes the believer and immerses him into the body of Christ.

In the baptism into the Holy Spirit, the Lord Jesus takes the believer and immerses him into the Holy Spirit. In the baptism into water, a disciple of the Lord Jesus takes the one who is converted and immerses him into water. We may spell it out as follows:

	BAPTISER	MEDIUM
Baptism into water	A disciple of the Lord Jesus	Water
Baptism into the Holy Spirit	The Lord Jesus	The Holy Spirit
Baptism into the body	The Holy Spirit	The body of Christ

In the baptism into the body, the Holy Spirit takes the believer and immerses him into the body of Christ. That is why no one can join the body of Christ on his own. The Holy Spirit must take him and immerse him into the body. Immediately someone is converted, the Holy Spirit takes him, and plunges him into the body of Christ.

May I clarify that joining a local assembly is not synonymous to being baptised into the body of Christ. You first become a member of the body, by the work of the Holy Spirit, then can you find and fit into a local church, where you meet the love of other children of God. The assembly of brethren is the body of Christ in its local expression.

Those who do not understand this think that if one is not baptised into the Holy Spirit, he does not belong to the church. No, it is not so. There is the resident Boss, the Holy Spirit, in every believer, doing His transforming work from inside. Some who are evidently not baptised or filled with the Holy Spirit can testify of transformations in their characters, because the Holy Spirit dwells within them.

At conversion, the Holy Spirit comes into the believer to work out the character of Christ in him. At baptism into the Holy Spirit, the Holy Spirit comes into the believer to give power for service. The baptism into the Holy Spirit has to do with power for service. The Lord told the disciples that they were to receive power, when the Holy Spirit comes upon them, and then they would be His witnesses.

46

ONE GOD AND FATHER OF US ALL

*A*ll believers have the same Father. No unbeliever has the same father as any believer. In our sonship to the Father, no unbeliever has a share. Their father is the devil. We believers have one Father, God the Father.

In Germany, a brother in Christ introduced his brother in the flesh, who had not believed as, "This is my brother, one mother." He wanted me to understand that they did not have the same Father. His brother was still an unbeliever.

All believers have one Father, God, who is above all, through all and in all.

CHAPTER EIGHT

But grace was given to each of us according to the measure of Christ's gift. Therefore it is said, 'When he ascended on high he led a host of captives, and he gave gifts to men' (In saying, 'He ascended,' what does it mean but that he had also descended into the lower parts of the earth? He who descended is he who also ascended far above all the heavens, that he might fill all things.) And his gifts were that some should be apostles, some prophets, some evangelists, some pastors and teachers, to equip the saints for the work of the ministry, for building up the body of Christ, until we all attain to the unity of the faith and of the knowledge of the Son of God, to mature manhood, to the measure of the stature of the fullness of Christ; so that we may no longer be children, tossed to and fro and carried about with every wind of doctrine, by the cunning of men, by their craftiness in deceitful wiles. Rather, speaking the truth in love, we are to grow into every way into him who is the head, into Christ, from whom the whole body, joined and knit together by every joint with which it is supplied, when each part is working properly, makes bodily growth and up builds itself in love.

— EPHESIANS 4:7-16

GRACE AND FREEDOM IN CHRIST

We have received grace according to the measure of Christ's gift. This means that there is limitless grace for all our needs. When all else fails, the grace of God is always there.

Furthermore, the apostle mentions the fact that when Christ ascended on high, He led a host of captives. Those captives were you and I. The devil had the keys of death, but when Jesus died, He went to the underworld, knocked out the devil, got the keys and led us out. He set us free, and on going to heaven, He led the host of captives whom we were, to freedom. Note that He did not only set us free. He ascended with us. That is why we are seated on the throne with Him.

HE GAVE GIFTS TO MEN

When the Lord led us as captives, and seated us with Him in heavenly places, He gave us gifts. The gifts here are principally with regards to the ministry of the word. They are as follows:

1. Apostles,
2. Prophets,
3. Evangelists,
4. Pastors and
5. Teachers.

Of course, there are other types of gifts, but the apostle here is concerned with gifts of men. The greatest gifts of God to the church are the gifts of men, of ministers or servants. Those are the most crucial gifts of God to the church, upon which she depends for progress.

These gifts were given:

1. To equip the saints for the work of the ministry,
2. For building up the body of Christ, until we all attain to the unity of the faith and of the knowledge of the Son of God, to mature manhood, to the measure of the stature of the fullness of Christ.

The apostles, prophets, evangelists, pastors and teachers were not to do the work of the ministry. Their task was to equip the saints for the work of the ministry. The work of the ministry has been assigned to the saints. This brings us to confront a serious problem that has hindered the church for a very long time.

Beginning from Catholicism, running through Protestantism and now in Pentecostalism, the work of the ministry has been shifted on to the apostles, prophets, evangelists, pastors and teachers. In God's purpose, the work of the ministry was meant for the saints, for the laity as some call it. But it has turned out to be confined to those who call themselves the clergy. This is certainly one of the devil's far-reaching distortions. May the church come out of this tragedy!

This has meant that the work of the ministry has fallen back into the hands of a very few lot of people, who do it more often to earn their bread than not. It was never in God's purpose to partition the church into the clergy and laity. It is of the wicked one. The situation is such that there are one or two people called pastors, who do all the work. They visit the sick, bury the dead, carry out baptism, preach and so on. If they are not there, nothing happens. It has also meant that the pastors must have some qualification, which is not a gift received from the Lord, but a certificate from some school.

He may be a young believer. But because he has a certificate from a certain school, he lords it over men and women of great maturity. He may be a pastor or not by ministry, but he is given that title and expected to function in that capacity. Very often, he must also be the teacher, evangelist and lord of many other things.

Those who have been specially gifted as apostles, prophets, evangelists, pastors and teachers are there to train the saints for the work of ministry and to build the body of Christ to maturity. The saints are to do all the work, all the work of the ministry. The building up of the body of Christ is for all the saints. They are to:

1. Lead people to the Lord,
2. Baptise them and,
3. Build them up according to Christ,
4. Labour to present the saved mature in Christ,

5. Protect them from the wicked one,
6. Protect them from false doctrines.
7. and so on.

The work of the ministry is the work of all the saints. Since this large body became a crowd of spectator, a lot of harm has been done to the church. No persons are to fold their arms and sit down because there is a pastor who does everything. It is not the pastors' business to run about praying for the sick. There is only an exceptional case where the elders are called upon to carry out the ministry of praying for the sick. This has to do with sickness that has come as a result of sin. You find this special circumstance in James chapter five.

The world is not yet all won to Christ because of this tragedy—that a few people mistakenly thought that the work of the ministry was theirs. Consequently, a great portion of the workers was made to constitute a spectator lot. The church, unfortunately, has become something of a football match, where thousands of people watch twenty-two people do the work. No! The thousands in the church ought to do the work, coached by the "twenty-two!"

Are you only a lay brother in church? Forget the distortions that have taken place. You owe it to Christ to ensure that you do the work of the ministry. Ministry is your responsibility. You will answer to God for it. If you are a spectator, and believe that there are some special persons to do the work of the ministry, you frustrate the very purpose of God.

I met someone somewhere who said, "Our church cannot go anywhere. They have not yet sent us a pastor." A gentleman told me of an assembly in one of the Pentecostal churches in my country, where the believers had not broken bread for six months, because although there was a pastor, he had not attained the rank in his church, that qualified him to minister communion. In that same church, people who were ready for baptism had to wait for four months because the big, big pastor had not yet come.

In the system which I came out of, my father told me that one reason why catechumen classes went on for three years was to allow enough time for the pastor to be able to visit. There was a time when there were only two pastors for the whole region where I come from. The greater difficulty was that they all did their travelling on foot. You can imagine how long people had to wait.

If you never hear it again, you have at least read it today, that the work of the ministry is the work of the saints. You are in the ministry. The only persons who are not in the ministry are those who are outside of Christ, that is, the unbelievers. All believers are in the ministry. If you do not exercise your ministry, you are fail God.

You are a servant of God, a full-time servant of God; your work goes on twenty-four hours a day. Wake up from sleep and accomplish your ministry. God has called you into ministry by calling you to Christ. Do not wait for anybody to do it for you. He will not do it. Or rather, even if he wanted to, he is not able to do his part of the ministry and do your own. Do not betray your ministry. You are responsible for the building up of the body of Christ.

The work of the ministry is so big that every believer must be putting in all that he has, and all of his ability, to build up the body of Christ.

UNITY OF THE FAITH, KNOWLEDGE OF THE SON

There must be apostles, prophets, evangelists, pastors and teachers until we all attain to the unity of the faith and of the knowledge of the Son of God, to mature manhood, to the measure of the stature of the fullness of Christ. Evidently, we have not yet reached there. Therefore, we must continue to have them.

I say this because some persons are mistakenly holding that the time of the apostles and prophets has gone by. On the contrary, these must be there in greater numbers, and labour until we all come to unity in the knowledge of the Son of God, and to mature manhood in Christ. What it means is that if you eliminate the apostles, prophets, evangelists, pastors and teachers, the whole thing will fall through.

In the wisdom of God, He saw that these five ministers were able to equip the saints for the ministry and to lead them to the full maturity that God wanted. You cannot do away with the gifted ministers without frustrating the purpose of God. But when the church will come to its full stature in Christ Jesus, not one of them will be needed.

CHILDREN, TOSSED TO AND FRO

These gifts are to exist so that we may no longer be children, tossed to and fro and carried about with every wind of doctrine, by the cunning of men, by their craftiness in deceitful wiles. The ministers are to ensure that the believers are stable. Where these ministers fail, people will be tossed about with every wind of doctrine. Some believers are easily carried away by every new lie. They are not stable in the Lord. They are still children. May the Lord grant them to grow, under the labours of the apostles, prophets, evangelists, pastors and teachers.

EACH PART WORKING PROPERLY

*I*t is important that there be parts in the body, but more, that they function properly. Every part must therefore develop itself to the maximum, so as to function at its best. For example, Paul said,

> *I worked harder than any of them, though it was not I, but the grace of God which is with me* (1 Corinthians 15:10).

Everyone is to labour to ensure that the body works properly, by putting in all they are and have to the full. There must be no spectators or idle persons in the church. Everybody must be working and putting in everything.

THE SOVEREIGN CHOICES OF GOD

*A*postle, prophet, evangelist, pastor or teacher, are gifts. The teacher is in no way inferior to the apostle. These gifts are not virtues. They are not merited. Paul did nothing to merit being called an apostle. He was called to be an apostle right from his mother's womb. The apostles whom the Lord Jesus called had nothing more than those who were not called. He chose twelve, who were not the greatest, who were not the best, and appointed them to be apostles. It was the sovereign choice of God.

The gifts too, are according to the sovereign choice of God. You cannot make yourself an apostle, prophet, evangelist, pastor or teacher. None of the gifts is greater than the other. One is not a teacher because he has not made as much spiritual progress as the pastor, or has not made as much progress as the evangelist, or has not made as much progress as the prophet, or has not made as much spiritual progress as the apostle.

It is God who places men in these ministries. If God makes you an apostle, it is a gift of God. If you are made a prophet, evangelist, pastor or teacher, it is the gift of God. You have, by this gift, been charged to equip the saints for ministry. It is not cause for boasting and lording it over the others.

MINISTRY PRIORITIES

*J*f you are made an apostle, a lot will be demanded of you. Your judgement will be more severe. Those to whom much has been given, much too will be demanded of them. James even says,

Let not many of you become teachers, my brethren, for you know that we who teach shall be judged with greater strictness (James 3: 1).

Should one boast of that which will procure him more judgement? Being gifted is a call to serve, with the knowledge that judgement is awaiting at the other end.

The only joy of the minister, ministering in any of the five dimensions, is that the saints are being prepared for the work of the ministry, and that the heart of God is being satisfied.

Do not leave the ministry God has given you, to cause confusion elsewhere. If your primary calling from God is to be a pastor, you must never sacrifice pasturing for anything else. The teacher must never sacrifice teaching or the evangelist sacrifice evangelism for anything.[1] If you are an apostle or prophet, ensure that nothing distracts you from apostle-work and prophesying respectively. Exercise your ministry.

When the body of Christ functions normally, the exercise of gifts is not by trial and error. It will be obvious that church-planting belongs to the apostles. Public evangelism should be carried out by the evangelists. Spiritual maturity does not transform someone into an evangelist. Teaching should be done by those who have the gift of teaching. In such a body, the pastor is allowed to do his work. Those who have various ministries should exercise those ministries. It would be wrong to give everybody a chance to do what they are not gifted in.

In the body, you do not vote for the pastor. Also, the pastor is not the one who is the most educated or has gone to some Bible school. Bible schools do not impart spiritual gifts. Ministry is given by the Lord; not by a school.

As it is obvious, Paul said he was an apostle, a preacher and a teacher. Barnabas and Paul were prophet-teachers in the church in Antioch before they were sent out on missionary work. Even after their missionary journeys, they came back to the church in Antioch and carried out the teaching ministry alongside the others. Normally, an apostle can carry out all the ministries, because he has passed through them.

The church is to labour with God, so that all the ministries are manifest. She must not accept the absence of any of the ministries. If one of the ministries is lacking, it is an abnormality that has to be corrected.

54

THE REST OF THE BODY

*W*hat if you are neither an apostle, a prophet, an evangelist, a pastor or a teacher? It means that you should be equipped by these to carry out the work of the ministry. As I have already said, it falls back on you to lead people to Christ, build them up, teach them, strengthen them, and so on. What it actually means is that the bulk of the work falls back on you. Far be it from you, to fold your arms and do nothing! Arise, dear saint, and get down to work. The Lord bless you as you do your own share of the work. Remember, your reward lies ahead.

CHAPTER NINE

Now this I affirm and testify in the Lord, that you must no longer live as the Gentiles do, in the futility of their minds; they are darkened in their understanding, alienated from the life of God because of the ignorance that is in them, due to their hardness of heart; they have become callous and have given themselves up to licentiousness, greedy to practise every kind of uncleanness. You did not so learn Christ -assuming that you have heard about him and were taught in him, as the truth is in Jesus. Put off your old nature which belongs to your former manner of life and is corrupt through deceitful lusts, and be renewed in the spirit of your minds, and put on the new nature, created after the likeness of God in true righteousness and holiness.

Therefore, putting away falsehood let everyone speak the truth with his neighbour, for we are members of one another. Be angry but do not sin; do not let the sun go down on your anger, and give no opportunity to the devil. Let the thief no longer steal, but rather let him labour, doing honest work with his hands, so that he may be able to give to those in need. Let no evil talk come out of your mouths, but only such as is good for edifying, as fits the occasion, that it may impart grace to those who hear. And do not grieve the Holy Spirit of God, in whom you were sealed for the day of redemption. Let all bitterness and wrath and anger and clamour and slander be put away from you, with all malice, and be kind to one another, tender-hearted, forgiving one another, as God in Christ forgave you.

— **EPHESIANS** 4:17-32

55

WE MUST NO LONGER LIVE AS THE GENTILES DO - 1

*W*ho are the Gentiles? How do they live? Gentiles are non-Jews. But in this context, they are all those who are outside of Christ. All those who are outside of Christ live in the futility of their minds. In Romans 1:21-23, Paul talks of those who

> *became futile in their thinking and their senseless minds were darkened. Claiming to be wise, they become fools, and exchanged the glory of the immortal God for images resembling mortal man or birds or animals or reptiles.*

Unbelievers are darkened in their understanding. They may solve very complicated equations and design vehicles that fly to the moon; but in reality, their minds are darkened.

Their minds are darkened with regards to the Lord. They are alienated from the life of God. Once a person is separated from the Lord, his mind is darkened. We do not only become darkened in our minds. We are all born with darkened minds, separated from the life of God. We are born alienated from the life of God.

We are born with profound ignorance of God even if we pretend to know. Many people are ignorant about the Bible although they pretend to know it. If you do not know the Lord Jesus Christ, you are ignorant. Without the knowledge of the Lord Jesus Christ, all that a man may know amounts to nothing. You may have a doctorate in mathematics, in law, medicine and in philosophy. But if you do not know the Lord Jesus Christ, your doctorates amount to nothing spiritually. You score nought with regard to spiritual knowledge.

You could be a doctor in theology without the knowledge that comes from the Lord Jesus Christ. That leaves you as ignorant as the rest without Christ. Why the ignorance? Because of the hardness of your heart. When this ignorance is not acknowledged, the heart becomes harder all the more. When the darkened, ignorant heart further pretends to be wise, it becomes foolish.

The first time a person hears the preaching of the gospel of salvation, the light of God shines through him. Often, he also immediately sees what it will cost to follow Christ. He faces the practical repercussions. He may find that he has to acknowledge that he was mistaken, do away with his idols, change his life-style and manner of thinking. Faced with these, he may either embrace Christ or say, "No," to Him. If he embraces Christ, he comes into His light. If he does not, he plunges into greater darkness.

The problem with many is not intellectual. They understand the gospel very well, but faced with the practical implications, they step back. The deep problem is not that they do not understand, or that there are contradictions in the Bible, or that there are many religions etc. They may philosophise and say all sorts of things, provided they keep the gospel away. When they have a problem, they turn to sorcery, a dark art, which they cannot explain intellectually.

The ease with which intellectuals turn to sorcery is a thing I cannot understand. But when faced with the gospel, they resort to logic. As a matter of fact, what is the logic in sorcery? Ultimately, the problem is moral. I have hardly met people with intellectual problems in relation to the gospel. The demands of the gospel are far more moral than intellectual. The Gospel demands radical moral change.

56

A CALLOUS WORLD

*B*ecause of a negative attitude towards the gospel that begins from the mind and grips the whole life, unbelievers become callous. They lack human feelings. A certain man with a doctorate had a problem with his wife; he attacked her with his teeth. Some, with callous hearts kill a baby in the womb. Some, well paid, in positions of authority, harden their hearts and ask for bribes from the poor and suffering. They do not ask where the poor persons will get the money from. They lack human feelings towards other people. Their hearts are hardened.

Think of a teacher who is so callous that a five percent pass or less— of his class of many students means nothing to him. Some even think that the higher the failure rate, the tougher they and their subjects are. They care nothing about the progress of the students and the loss of time involved. In a general way, the world is becoming increasingly callous. Women afford to poison or knife their husbands and vice versa. They forget the intimacy and maybe the children they have had together. How could all of the past be forgotten in a moment of anger?

In addition to being callous, the unbeliever gives himself to licentiousness. They just do horrible things. They are greedy to carry out every sort of unclean things. It looks like a deliberate commitment to carry out anything unclean. The Bible talks of men who no longer want women and vice versa. They have advanced so much in their sin that they want same-sex sexual relationships. Things have gone so bad that some countries have made homosexuality a nationally accepted and legalised practice. Some pastors, the devil's pastors, bless homosexual marriages. It now seems as if the greater a sin, the greater the man who commits it. The present world is very much ripe for God's judgement.

57

WE MUST NO LONGER LIVE AS THE GENTILES DO - 2

*T*he apostle warned that the believer must no longer live as the gentiles do. Why did he have to warn against such living? Because it is possible that a believer falls back to such living. From my observation, many Christians are also becoming callous. They are emotionally harder and more difficult to reach out to.

Could it be that you gave someone your love, it was rejected and then you hardened your heart towards that man or woman and kept your distance? Could it be that from one man or woman you generalised your hardness of heart to all men or women? Have you become simply hard? If yes, then you too, are callous, and living like the gentiles do. God forbids it!

Someone let you down and you felt bad. Is that the reason for which you have decided to trust no one anymore? You have hardened your heart to all. You have become callous! Did not Jesus trust Peter who betrayed him, and even make him leader of his people afterwards? Do you see in Christ a callous heart? Did He reject those who let Him down? Did not all the disciples abandon Him and run away? Did he not go looking for them afterwards? Where then are your grounds for developing a callous attitude?

Is there a justification for building a wall around your heart for self-protection? Did the Lord protect Himself that way? Did He not keep His heart open to Judas for more than three years even though He knew Judas would betray Him? Did the Lord not love him right to the end? Dear saint, break free from your callous heart and begin to flow in love again.

Should such walls be built in the name of the Lord Jesus Christ? Should such be tolerated in the church of the first-born? Should it be in the church of the One who gave Himself away to all right to the end? Look at it this way – when did Jesus change His mind about loving you? If He were callous, would He even talk to you? Have you forgotten how often you have grieved Him? Did not His love always flow to you in an unchanging way?

You used to be warm, then something happened and you are now a frozen person. You are hard to those who love you and to those who are near you. You prefer distant relationships. Is your marriage breaking because you no longer give yourself away? How then do you hope to build a Christian home, in the name of the One who never withheld Himself? We know one thing about the love of the Lord Jesus Christ - it does not protect itself.

The callous of heart can only minister death. They do not know how to be sorry. They cannot lift up the emotionally downtrodden. They know no tears. Such could not have learnt it from the Lord Jesus Christ.

Someone said, "I will love you always, but my faith in you is broken forever." It is certainly no longer love because love always trusts. People run away from hurts and run away from all counselling that may make them involved. This is exactly what the Gentiles do. We Christians must not live like that.

58

YOU DID NOT LEARN SO FROM CHRIST

hat do you do when you see someone who is loving and trusting? Do you consider him a young fool who will soon learn? For many people, the older they grow, the harder and sadder they become. Are you one such? If you are, you are not living like Christ. It does not matter what has happened to you, or what people have done to you. You do not have a licence from the Lord to be callous. There is need for deep repentance and crying out to God that what has been destroyed by your callousness should be repaired.

- The callous have hurt the Lord deeply.
- The callous have hurt the church deeply.
- The callous have hurt their families deeply.
- The callous have hurt themselves deeply.

The callous have hurt their relationships deeply. It is very hard to live with a callous person, one who is not affected by whatever happens around. Would you not cry out to the Lord, "Lord, unbind me so that I might flow?"

I was in one city preaching the gospel. A lady came to see me. She had bought a very expensive gift for another sister. When she offered it, the sister said, "I have no peace in my heart to receive it." She had no peace, perhaps because she was already in pieces as a result of the hardness of her heart. She could no longer receive love. She suspected everything. That is not Christian.

The model to each one of us remains the Lord Jesus Christ. We must model our character to His. May we never justify a character fault in us on the basis of what we have suffered. Jesus went through all that He went through, but never renounced Himself. May we, too, never renounce Him in our character, whatever the reasons.

CHAPTER TEN

Therefore be imitators of God, as beloved children. And walk in love, as Christ loved us and gave himself up for us, a fragrant offering and sacrifice to God. But fornication and all impurity or covetousness must not even be named among you, as is fitting among saints. Let there be no filthiness, nor silly talk, nor levity, which are not fitting; but instead let there be thanksgiving. Be sure of this, that no fornicator or impure man, or one who is covetous (that is, an idolater), has any inheritance in the kingdom of Christ and of God. Let no one deceive you with empty words, for it is because of these things that the wrath of God comes upon the sons of disobedience. Therefore, do not associate with them, for once you were darkness, but now you are light in the Lord; walk as children of light (for the fruit of light is found in all that is good and right and true), and try to learn what is pleasing to the Lord. Take no part in the unfruitful works of darkness, but instead expose them. For it is a shame even to speak of the things that they do in secret; but when anything is exposed by the light it becomes visible, for anything that becomes visible is light. Therefore, it is said, 'Awake, O sleeper, and arise from the dead, and Christ shall give you light.'

Look carefully then how you walk, not as unwise men but as wise, making the most of the time, because the days are evil. Therefore do not be foolish, but understand what the will of the Lord is. And do not get drunk with wine, for that is debauchery; but be filled with the Spirit, addressing one another in psalms and hymns and spiritual songs, singing and making melody to the Lord with all y our heart, always and for everything giving thanks in the name of our Lord Jesus Christ to God the Father.

— EPHESIANS 5 1-20

59

WALKING IN LOVE - 1

*W*e have been called to walk in love. The apostle insists;
Let all bitterness and wrath and anger and clamour and slander be put
away from you, with all malice, and be kind to one another,
tender-hearted, forgiving one another, as God in Christ forgave
you (Ephesians 4:31-32).

This is a command to be obeyed, and, it is as binding as all the other commandments. The following must be put away:

- Bitterness,
- Wrath,
- Anger,
- Clamour,
- Slander and
- Malice.

In their place the following must be put on:

- Kindness towards one another,
- Tender-heartedness and
- Mutual forgiveness.

Many believers have bitter hearts and yet participate in the table of the Lord. This can only be done to their undoing. You keep sin in your heart only to your own undoing. Regardless of what someone has done to you, the sun must not set on your anger. It is even worse for a believer to be bitter against an unbeliever. How will he then preach the salvation of Christ to him? What about being bitter against your brother in Christ? It is like being bitter against yourself.

The following things must also be put away because they grieve the Spirit of the Lord:

1. Envy
2. Resentment
3. Revenge
4. Criticism
5. Intolerance
6. Hatred
7. Jealousy
8. Gossip
9. Sarcasm
10. An unforgiving spirit

Because of the presence of these sins in the hearts of many believers, they cannot be baptised into the Holy Spirit. For those who were already baptised before letting in these sins into their hearts, they cannot know the power of the Holy Spirit. More often than never, these sins are not treated with the gravity that they deserve. Yet, they very much grieve the Spirit of the Lord.

Do you find yourself trapped in any or all of these sins? Are you the very embodiment of bitterness and resentment? Can anything done by another person be good in your eyes? Are you expecting the worst to happen? Must you always find fault? Must you always have an eye for that which will go wrong?

A gossiper, slanderer or bitter person is in a decaying condition. He is deteriorating. He cannot be wishing people evil and be blessed. He will reap what he has sown. The Lord said to Abraham,

I will bless those who bless you, and him who curses you I will curse...
   (Genesis 12:3).

Since believers are the sons of Abraham by faith, you curse them to your own undoing, or bless them for your own good.

Could it be that you are under the weight of the curses you have been releasing against the children of Abraham? Does it explain why many things about you are not working? Why are your friendships, relationships and marriage breaking? Could the reason be found in your prophetic attitude towards believers? Can one who curses the children of God and is bitter towards them make spiritual progress? Have you made spiritual progress?

It is easier to take time and stop these sins, than spend hours upon hours praying prayers that will not be answered by the God of Abraham. Prayer and fasting will not secure forgiveness for sin that must be acknowledged, repented of and forsaken. The baptism into the Holy Spirit will not come to cover un-confessed and un-forsaken sins. Except it is a prayer of repentance, or a fast to weep before God for forgiveness, all else that is done with sin in the heart is vain.

WALKING IN LOVE - 2

*T*he apostle demands that among believers the following must not exist:

- Filthiness,
- Silly talk and
- Levity.

You should not be the one who takes silly talk around. A lot of the talking of many brethren is silly talk. It is silly talk when one speaks only to while away the time, or when the words are not fitting. There must be nothing frivolous about the believer. Frivolous relationships and letter-writing will not be tolerated before God.

The Christian is a purposeful person. His relationships are with a purpose. Let me ask you - do your relationships have a purpose? What kind of relationships are you entertaining now? Where will they lead you to, when fully developed?

THANKSGIVING TO THE LORD

he Bible recommends that after we have put away filthiness, silly talk and levity, we should pre-occupy ourselves with giving thanks to the Lord. It is a terrible thing to have two, three or more believers gather around to gossip, or to listen to complaints against some person or the other! Such is not fitting for the saints. You must not partake of such activity, nor should you let anyone who names the name of the Lord do such evil. Rather, when we meet, two, three or more, let thanksgiving rise up to the Lord our God.

We must, always, for everything, give thanks to the Lord. Before you complain about your wife, or husband, first stop and give thanks to the Lord for her or for him. Before you hoot at another road-user in anger, first thank the Lord for him. Be a thankful person. Let us be a thankful people, and the name of the Lord will be glorified.

PURITY OF HEART

*T*he Bible says,

But fornication and all impurity or covetousness must not even be named among you, as is fitting among saints (Ephesians 5:3).

When the apostle says this, it could mean that there were some in the church at Ephesus who were practising such works of darkness. Such have no inheritance in the kingdom of God:

Be sure of this, that no fornicator or impure man, or one who is covetous (that is, an idolater), has any inheritance in the kingdom of Christ and of God (Ephesians 5:5).

If you are a fornicator, or impure person, you have no place in the kingdom of God. Unless you repent radically and forsake your fornication, you have no part in God and no place in heaven.

No fornicator has the salvation of God. From what has he been saved? He is still wallowing in fornication! To such, the apostle says,

Let no one deceive you with empty words, for it is because of these things that the wrath of God comes upon the sons of disobedience (Ephesians 5:6).

The fornicator has no place in God and in the church of the first-born. He cannot lift up holy hands to the Lord in the assembly of the saints, because his hands are soiled with impurity.

How is it with your mind? If your mind is impure, your heart is no better. God looks at the heart and takes note of what is there. Are your thoughts like those of a fornicator or an adulterer's? Such cannot be filled with the Holy Spirit of God. Could it be that instead of being filled with the Holy Spirit of God, you are filled with sexual immorality or with covetousness?

Are you the one who causes people to lust? Do you provoke immoral thoughts in others? If yes, then you are a stumbling block. If your dressing leads people to sin, you have participated in their sin. Something is equally wrong in your own walk with God. Many women followed the Lord Jesus Christ. Who of them lusted after Him? They could not: His presence imposed the holiness of God. Spiritual men and spiritual women provoke purity in the hearts of those around them. But carnal men and women stir up carnal desires.

63

WALKING AS CHILDREN OF LIGHT

*T*he Bible says,

Therefore, do not associate with them, for once you were darkness, but now you are light in the Lord; walk as children of light (for the fruit of light is found in all that is good and right and true), and try to learn what is pleasing to the Lord (Ephesians 5:7).

You must not associate with those who abide in the works of darkness. You have had a radical turn from darkness to light. You just must be pure. You must labour for the holiness without which no one will see God. The Bible says,

Blessed are the pure in heart: for they shall see God (Matthew 5:8, KJV).

The impure in heart will not see Him. Are you pure in heart?

What is God's evaluation of your heart?

One characteristic of the modern Pentecostal movement is that it has focused on spiritual gifts without holiness. Normally, there has to be purity before there is spiritual power. Being gifted in sin is to be gifted to one's undoing. The manifestations of spiritual gifts and power, without holiness, are deceptive. When the pure in heart have spiritual gifts and manifest spiritual power, the kingdom of God is advanced. But the power of gifts will never substitute for God's demands for purity.

The pure in heart are also the pure in mind. Without purity of mind, there can be no purity of heart. If the thoughts are dirty, the heart is also dirty. The only recourse for such is in repentance and cleansing from sin. God will not cover His eyes to sin and fill people with the Holy Spirit. The Holy Spirit is for those who are walking in the light of God. It is for the children of light.

The apostle demands that we take no part in the unfruitful works of darkness, but instead expose them. Gossip is a work of darkness. It is to be exposed. Many have committed sins which they would be delivered of if they exposed them. Are you in the bondage of some sin or sinful practice? Unless you expose it and seek to be delivered, you will remain in its grip forever.

64

REDEEMING THE TIME

*T*he Bible says,

Awake, O sleeper, and arise from the dead, and Christ shall give you light.

Wake up from your sin and backsliding. Wake up with regard to your Bible reading, giving to the Lord, evangelism and so on. Get back your life to focus. Ensure that you are not wasting time through purposeless visits, shopping and chatting.

Where is your commitment to redeem the time? Someone prayed, "O Lord, help me to use this day properly, because I am meeting it for the first time today, and the next time I meet it, it will be on Judgment Day." You ought to pray the same because you are meeting this hour now, and will only meet it again before the Judgment Seat of Christ. We shall all appear before the Judgment Seat of Christ to give account of our lives,

- Years,
- Months,
- Weeks,
- Days,
- Hours and of our
- Minutes.

If the sun were late for ten minutes, there would be chaos among the heavenly bodies. But we are greater than the sun. If fifteen minutes of lateness are of far-reaching consequences, then fifteen wasted minutes for the believer are tragic beyond telling. What then about a wasted day, weekend or a wasted week?

65

FILLED WITH THE HOLY SPIRIT

he Holy Spirit is the Spirit of holiness. We are to be possessed with the Holy Spirit in the same manner in which wine possesses drunks. All drunkards are happy when under the control of alcohol. In like manner, believers who are filled with the Holy Spirit are joyful. While the joy of wine ends up in sadness, the joy of the Holy Spirit wells up to greater joy and happiness.

The sadness of your life may be a testimony of a life that is not filled with the Holy Spirit. When one is filled 'with the Holy Spirit, he also enjoys the peace of the Lord. When there is no peace, then something is wrong, and needs to be put right.

Spirit-filled people address one another in psalms and hymns and spiritual songs, singing and making melody to the Lord with all their hearts. Always and for everything, they give thanks in the name of our Lord Jesus Christ to God the Father.

Most drunkards sing and make melody to the glory of the devil. Those filled with the Holy Spirit also sing and make melody to the Lord Jesus Christ. Spiritual songs come out of Spirit-filled believers. Once I went to a church in the USA and the believers were singing. They were totally taken up with their performance. It was as if they were drugged. Everything in them was involved. They had become one with what they were singing. That is what I am talking about.

But one finds the contrary in may places around. There is no evidence of a Lord that has captured and possessed the believers. They do not sing with all their hearts. They hold back and would not betray their emotions. But it is not the same thing when the same people are angry. They keep their emotions for anger, but will not emotionally flow to the Lord of Lords.

Go watch what happens in football stadiums, then go back to church. What do you find in most cases? Most churches are dead, compared to the life we generally find in the stadiums. The people are dead towards God but alive towards the world and the things of the world.

Finally,

> ...Be filled with the Holy Spirit, addressing one another in psalms and hymns and spiritual songs, singing and making melody to the Lord with all your heart, always and for everything giving thanks in the name of our Lord Jesus Christ to God the Father (Ephesians 5:18b-20).

Amen.

VERY IMPORTANT!!!

If you have not yet received Jesus as your Lord and Saviour, I encourage you to receive Him. Here are some steps to help you,

ADMIT that you are a sinner by nature and by practice and that on your own you are without hope. Tell God you have personally sinned against Him in your thoughts, words and deeds. Confess your sins to Him, one after another in a sincere prayer. Do not leave out any sins that you can remember. Truly turn from your sinful ways and abandon them. If you stole, steal no more. If you have been committing adultery or fornication, stop it. God will not forgive you if you have no desire to stop sinning in all areas of your life, but if you are sincere, He will give you the power to stop sinning.

BELIEVE that Jesus Christ, who is God's Son, is the only Way, the only Truth and the only Life. Jesus said,

> *"I am the way, the truth and the life; no one comes to the Father, but by me" (John 14:6).*

The Bible says,

> *"For there is one God, and there is one mediator between God and men, the man Christ Jesus, who gave himself as a ransom for all" (1 Timothy 2:5-6).*

"And there is salvation in no one else (apart from Jesus), for there is no other name under heaven given among men by which we must be saved" (Acts 4:12).

But to all who received him, who believed in his name, he gave power to become children of God..." (John 1:12).

BUT,

CONSIDER the cost of following Him. Jesus said that all who follow Him must deny themselves, and this includes selfish financial, social and other interests. He also wants His followers to take up their crosses and follow Him. Are you prepared to abandon your own interests daily for those of Christ? Are you prepared to be led in a new direction by Him? Are you prepared to suffer for Him and die for Him if need be? Jesus will have nothing to do with half-hearted people. His demands are total. He will only receive and forgive those who are prepared to follow Him AT ANY COST. Think about it and count the cost. If you are prepared to follow Him, come what may, then there is something to do.

INVITE Jesus to come into your heart and life. He says,

"Behold I stand at the door and knock. If anyone hears my voice and opens the door (to his heart and life), I will come in to him and eat with him, and he with me " (Revelation 3:20).

Why don't you pray a prayer like the following one or one of your own construction as the Holy Spirit leads?

"Lord Jesus, I am a wretched, lost sinner who has sinned in thought, word and deed. Forgive all my sins and cleanse me. Receive me, Saviour and transform me into a child of God. Come into my heart now and give me eternal life right now. I will follow you at all costs, trusting the Holy Spirit to give me all the power I need."

When you pray this prayer sincerely, Jesus answers at once and justifies you before God and makes you His child.

*Please write to us (**ztfbooks@cmfionline.org**) and I will pray for you and help you as you go on with Jesus Christ.*

THANK YOU

For Reading This Book

If you have any question and/or need help, do not hesitate to contact us through **ztfbooks@cmfionline.org**. If the book has blessed you, then we would also be grateful if you leave a positive review at your favorite retailer.

ZTF BOOKS, through Christian Publishing House (CPH) offers a wide selection of best selling Christian books (in print, eBook & audiobook formats) on a broad spectrum of topics, including marriage & family, sexuality, practical spiritual warfare, Christian service, Christian leadership, and much more. Visit us at **ztfbooks.com** to learn more about our latest releases and special offers. **And thank you for being a ZTF BOOK reader**.

We invite you to connect with more from the author through social media (**cmfionline**) and/or ministry website (**ztfministry.org**), where we offer both on-ground and remote training courses (all year round) from basic to university level at the **University of Prayer and Fasting (WUPF)** and the **School of Knowing and Serving God (SKSG)**. You are highly welcome to enrol at your soonest convenience. A **FREE online Bible Course** is also available.

Finally, we would like to recommend to you another book in this series Leading A Local Church:

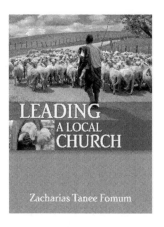

This book "Leading a Local Church" is a compilation of the teaching of Professor Zacharias Tanee Fomum addressed to the saints in Yaoundé, Cameroon during a leadership training course. This book presents what it takes to lead a local church and what leadership is. The author explains the critical place of having a goal geared towards the saving of the lost in the building of a local church. The method for the accomplishment of the goal is the making of disciples.

When a shepherd leaves the flock just for a day in pursuit of gain, he has put a knife into his heart and things will never be the same afterwards. A shepherd who loves the world has lost God, has lost the vision and has betrayed the sheep. According to the author the spiritual gift of leadership is the unusual ability to produce other leaders. The leader is the one who takes risks and break new grounds. Leadership is a call to provide a model.

Dear reader, we recommend this book to you while praying that the Lord will use it to make of you a leader who has put on God enough to be able to lead a local church and raise others of his kind.

ABOUT THE AUTHOR

Professor Zacharias Tanee Fomum was born in the flesh on 20th June 1945 and became born again on 13th June 1956. On 1st October 1966, He consecrated his life to the Lord Jesus and to His service, and was filled with the Holy Spirit on 24th October 1970. He was taken to be with the Lord on 14th March, 2009.

Pr Fomum was admitted to a first class in the Bachelor of Science degree, graduating as a prize winning student from Fourah Bay College in the University of Sierra Leone in October 1969. At the age of 28, he was awarded a Ph.D. in Organic Chemistry by the University of Makerere, Kampala in Uganda. In October 2005, he was awarded a Doctor of Science (D.Sc) by the University of Durham, Great Britain. This higher doctorate was in recognition of his distinct contributions to scientific knowledge through research. As a Professor of Organic Chemistry in the University of Yaoundé 1, Cameroon, Professor Fomum supervised or co-supervised more than 100 Master's Degree and Doctoral Degree theses and co-authored over 160 scientific articles in leading international journals. He considered Jesus Christ the Lord of Science ("For by Him all things were created..." – Colossians 1:16), and scientific research an act of obedience to God's command to "subdue the earth" (Genesis 1:28). He therefore made the Lord Jesus the Director of his research laboratory while he took the place of deputy director, and attributed his outstanding success as a scientist to Jesus' revelational leadership.

In more than 40 years of Christian ministry, Pr Fomum travelled extensively, preaching the Gospel, planting churches and training spiritual leaders. He made more than:

- 700 missionary journeys within Cameroon, which ranged from one day to three weeks in duration.
- 500 missionary journeys to more than 70 different nations in all the six continents. These ranged from two days to six weeks in duration.

By the time of his going to be with the Lord in 2009, he had preached in over 1000 localities in Cameroon, sent over 200 national missionaries into many localities in Cameroon and planted over 1300 churches in the various administrative provinces of Cameroon. At his base in Yaoundé, he planted and built a mega-church with his co-workers which grew to a steady membership of about 12,000. Pr Fomum was the founding team-leader of Christian Missionary Fellowship International (CMFI); an evangelism, soul-winning, disciple making, Church-planting and missionary-sending movement with more than 200 international missionaries and thousands of churches in 65 nations spread across Africa, Europe, the Americas, Asia and Oceania. In the course of their ministry, Pr Fomum and his team witnessed more than 10,000 recorded healing miracles performed by God in answer to prayer in the name of Jesus Christ. These miracles include instant healings of headaches, cancers, HIV/AIDS, blindness, deafness, dumbness, paralysis, madness, and new teeth and organs received.

Pr Fomum read the entire Bible more than 60 times, read more than 1350 books on the Christian faith and authored over 150 books to advance the Gospel of Jesus Christ. 5 million copies of these books are in circulation in 12 languages as well as 16 million gospel tracts in 17 languages.

Pr Fomum was a man who sought God. He spent between 15 minutes and six hours daily alone with God in what he called Daily Dynamic Encounters with God (DDEWG). During these DDEWG he read God's Word, meditated on it, listened to God's voice, heard God speak to him, recorded what God was saying to him and prayed it through. He thus had over 18,000 DDEWG. He also had over 60 periods of withdrawing to seek God alone for periods that ranged from 3 to 21 days (which he termed Retreats for Spiritual Progress). The time he spent seeking God slowly transformed him into a man who hungered, thirsted and panted after God. His unceasing heart cry was: "Oh, that I would have more of God!"

Pr Fomum was a man of prayer and a leading teacher on prayer in many churches and conferences around the world. He considered prayer to be the most important work that can be done for God and for man. He was a man of faith who believed that God answers prayer. He kept a record of his prayer requests and had over 50, 000 recorded answers to prayer in his prayer books. He carried out over 100 Prayer Walks of between five and forty-seven kilometres in towns and cities around the world. He and his team carried out over 57 Prayer Crusades (periods of forty days and nights during which at least eight hours are invested into prayer each day). They also carried out over 80 Prayer Sieges (times of near non-stop praying that ranges from 24 hours to 120 hours). He authored the Prayer Power Series, a 13-volume set of books on various aspects of prayer; Supplication, Fasting, Intercession and Spiritual Warfare. He started prayer chains, prayer rooms, prayer houses, national and continental prayer movements in Cameroon and other nations. He worked with leaders of local churches in India to disciple and train more than 2 million believers.

Pr Fomum also considered fasting as one of the weapons of Christian Spiritual Warfare. He carried out over 250 fasts ranging from three days to forty days, drinking only water or water supplemented with soluble vitamins. Called by the Lord to a distinct ministry of intercession, he pioneered fasting and prayer movements and led in battles against principalities and powers obstructing the progress of the Gospel and God's global purposes. He was enabled to carry out 3 supra – long fasts of between 52 and 70 days in his final years.

Pr Fomum chose a lifestyle of simplicity and "self- imposed poverty" in order to invest more funds into the critical work of evangelism, soul winning, church-planting and the building up of believers. Knowing the importance of money and its role in the battle to reach those without Christ with the glorious Gospel, he and his wife grew to investing 92.5% of their earned income from all sources (salaries, allowances, royalties and cash gifts) into the Gospel. They invested with the hope that, as they grew in the knowledge and the love of the Lord, and the perishing souls of people, they would one day invest 99% of their income into the Gospel.

He was married to Prisca Zei Fomum and they had seven children who are all involved in the work of the Gospel, some serving as missionaries. Prisca is a national and international minister, specializing in the winning and discipling of children to Jesus Christ. She also communicates and imparts the vision of ministry to children with a view to raising and building up ministers to them.

The Professor owed all that he was and all that God had done through him, to the unmerited favour and blessing of God and to his worldwide army of friends and co-workers. He considered himself nothing without them and the blessing of God; and would have amounted to nothing but for them. All praise and glory to Jesus Christ!

facebook.com/cmfionline

twitter.com/cmfionline

instagram.com/cmfionline

pinterest.com/cmfionline

youtube.com/cmfionline

ALSO BY Z.T. FOMUM

Online Catalog: https://ztfbooks.com

THE CHRISTIAN WAY

1. The Way Of Life
2. The Way Of Obedience
3. The Way Of Discipleship
4. The Way Of Sanctification
5. The Way Of Christian Character
6. The Way Of Spiritual Power
7. The Way Of Christian Service
8. The Way Of Spiritual Warfare
9. The Way Of Suffering For Christ
10. The Way Of Victorious Praying
11. The Way Of Overcomers
12. The Way Of Spiritual Encouragement
13. The Way Of Loving The Lord

THE PRAYER POWER SERIES

1. The Way Of Victorious Praying
2. The Ministry Of Fasting
3. The Art Of Intercession
4. The Practice Of Intercession
5. Praying With Power
6. Practical Spiritual Warfare Through Prayer
7. Moving God Through Prayer
8. The Ministry Of Praise And Thanksgiving
9. Waiting On The Lord In Prayer
10. The Ministry Of Supplication
11. Life-Changing Thoughts On Prayer, Volume 1
12. The Centrality Of Prayer

PRACTICAL HELPS FOR OVERCOMERS

GOD, SEX AND YOU

3. Enjoying The Married Life
4. **Divorce And Remarriage**
5. A Successful Marriage; The Husband's Making
6. A Successful Marriage; The Wife's Making

RECENT TITLES BY THE ZTF EDITORIAL TEAM

1. Power For Service
2. The Art Of Worship
3. Issues Of The Heart
4. In The Crucible For Service
5. Spiritual Nobility
6. Roots And Destinies
7. Revolutionary Thoughts On Spiritual Leadership
8. The Leader And His God
9. The Overthrow Of Principalities And Powers
10. Walking With God (Vol. 1)
11. God Centeredness
12. Victorious Dispositions
13. The Believer's Conscience
14. The Processes Of Faith
15. Spiritual Gifts
16. The Missionary As A Son
17. You, Your Team And Your Ministry
18. Prayer And A Walk With God
19. Leading A Local Church
20. Church Planting Strategies
21. The Character And The Personality of The Leader
22. Deliverance From The Sin of Gluttony
23. The Spirit Filled Life
24. The Church: Rights And Responsibilities Of The Believer
25. Thoughts On Marriage
26. Learning To Importune In Prayer
27. Jesus Saves And Heals Today
28. God, Money And You
29. Meet The Liberator
30. Salvation And Soul Winning

PRACTICAL HELPS IN SANCTIFICATION

MAKING SPIRITUAL PROGRESS

5. Brokenness: The Secret Of Spiritual Overflow
6. The Secret Of Spiritual Rest
7. Making Spiritual Progress, Volume 1
8. Making Spiritual Progress, Volume 2
9. Making Spiritual Progress, Volume 3
10. Making Spiritual Progress, Volume 4

EVANGELISM

1. God's Love And Forgiveness
2. The Way Of Life
3. Come Back Home My Son; I Still Love You
4. Jesus Loves You And Wants To Heal You
5. Come And See; Jesus Has Not Changed!
6. 36 Reasons For Winning The Lost To Christ
7. Soul Winning, Volume 1
8. Soul Winning, Volume 2
9. Celebrity A Mask

UNCATEGORISE

1. Laws Of Spiritual Success, Volume 1
2. The Shepherd And The Flock
3. Deliverance From Demons
4. Inner Healing
5. No Failure Needs To Be Final
6. Facing Life's Problems Victoriously
7. A Word To The Students
8. The Prophecy Of The Overthrow Of The Satanic Prince Of Cameroon
9. Basic Christian Leadership
10. A Missionary life and a missionary heart
11. Power to perform miracles

WOMEN OF THE GLORY

1. **The Secluded Worshipper**: The Life, Ministry, And Glorification Of The Prophetess Anna
2. **Unending Intimacy**: The Transformation, Choices And Overflow of Mary of Bethany
3. **Winning Love:** The rescue, development and fulfilment of Mary Magdalene
4. **Not Meant for Defeat**: The Rise, Battles, and Triumph of Queen Esther

ZTF COMPLETE WORKS

1. The School of Soul Winners and Soul Winning
2. The Complete Works of Zacharias Tanee Fomum on Prayer (Volume 1)
3. The Complete Works of Zacharias Tanee Fomum on Leadership (Volume 1)
4. The Complete Works of Z.T Fomum on Marriage
5. Making Spiritual Progress (The Complete Box Set of Four Volumes)

OTHER TITLES

1. A Broken Vessel
2. The Joy of Begging to Belong to the Lord Jesus Christ: A Testimony

ZTF AUTO-BIOGRAPHIES

1. From His Lips: About The Author
2. From His Lips: About His Co-Workers
3. From His Lips: Back From His Missions
4. From His Lips: About Our Ministry

DISTRIBUTORS OF ZTF BOOKS

These books can be obtained in French and English Language from any of the following distribution outlets:

EDITIONS DU LIVRE CHRETIEN (ELC)

- **Location:** Paris, France
- **Email:** editionlivrechretien@gmail.com
- **Phone:** +33 6 98 00 90 47

INTERNET

- **Location:** on all major online **eBook, Audiobook** and **print-on-demand** (paperback) retailers (Amazon, Google, iBooks, B&N, Ingram, NotionPress, etc.).
- **Email**: ztfbooks@cmfionline.org
- **Phone**: +47 454 12 804
- **Website**: ztfbooks.com

CPH YAOUNDE

- **Location:** Yaounde, Cameroon
- **Email:** editionsztf@gmail.com
- **Phone:** +237 74756559

ZTF LITERATURE AND MEDIA HOUSE

- **Location:** Lagos, Nigeria
- **Email:** zlmh@ztfministry.org
- **Phone:** +2348152163063

CPH BURUNDI

- **Location:** Bujumbura, Burundi
- **Email:** cph-burundi@ztfministry.org
- **Phone:** +257 79 97 72 75

CPH UGANDA

- **Location:** Kampala, Uganda
- **Email:** cph-uganda@ztfministry.org
- **Phone:** +256 785 619613

CPH SOUTH AFRICA

- **Location:** Johannesburg, RSA
- **Email:** tantohtantoh@yahoo.com
- **Phone**: +27 83 744 5682

NOTES

9. THE RICHES OF HIS GRACE

1. This is certainly no encouragement to anyone to go on sinning. God delivers from sin. He also sanctifies. But the reality of His grace lies in the fact that even if you went a million times, or a billion times, He will never say you have come too many times.

36. STRENGTHENED IN THE INNER MAN

1. Giving up one's rights.

53. MINISTRY PRIORITIES

1. If you have no burden for souls and are not leading people to Christ at a personal level, you cannot be an evangelist. An evangelist has an extra burden for the lost. Night and day, on his own, he labours for the lost. When he is on stage to preach, it is only a continuation of what he has been doing in private.

Printed in Great Britain
by Amazon